"This is easily one of the most innovative new cookbooks of the year. Joni Marie Newman has transformed the humble veggie burger into a culinary delight with endless possibilities. From the Middle East to the Far East and back to the spicy Southwest, prepare your burger-loving taste buds for some serious global trekking."

—ALISA FLEMING, founder of GoDairyFree.org and author of *Go Dairy Free: The Guide and Cookbook*

"Joni Marie Newman has done a brilliant service to animals, the Earth, and all of us with *The Best Veggie Burgers on the Planet*. A book of tantalizing, creative recipes, it rescues the burger and barbecue scene from jaded reruns of meat and cheese. With sumptuous color photos of a mouth-watering display of 101 burgers from around the world, it introduces fresh vistas to the already vast universe of vegan cookery. These delicious, healthy, and humane recipes are sure to rouse both vegans and non-vegans to rush to the kitchen and cook with new inspiration."

—DR. WILL TUTTLE, author of the best-selling *The World Peace Diet*

"If you think veggie burgers are boring, this book will be quite the eye-opener. The recipes are amazingly varied, delicious, and are filled with healthy plant-based foods. Most of them are simple to make. For many people, this could be the beginning of a real culinary adventure."

—JOHN ROBBINS, author of *The Food Revolution*, *Diet for a New America*, and many other bestsellers

THE BEST VEGGIE BURGERS ON THE PLANET

101 Globally inspired Vegan Creations Packed with
Fresh Flavors and Exciting New Tastes

JONI MARIE NEWMAN

Co-Author of *500 Vegan Recipes* and
The Complete Guide to Vegan Food Substitutions

FAIR WINDS
PRESS
BEVERLY, MASSACHUSETTS

Text © 2011 Joni Marie Newman
Photography © 2011 Rockport Publishers

First published in the USA in 2011 by
Fair Winds Press, a member of
Quayside Publishing Group
100 Cummings Center
Suite 406-L
Beverly, MA 01915-6101
www.fairwindspress.com

15 14 13 12 11   2 3 4 5

ISBN-13: 978-1-59233-476-6
ISBN-10: 1-59233-476-8

Digital edition published in 2011
eISBN-13: 978-1-61058-056-4

Library of Congress Cataloging-in-Publication Data
Newman, Joni-Marie.
101 globally inspired vegan creations packed with fresh flavors and exciting new tastes / Joni Marie
Newman ; with photography by Celine Steen.
     p. cm.
Includes index.
ISBN-13: 978-1-59233-476-6
ISBN-10: 1-59233-476-8
1. Meat substitutes. 2. Hamburgers. 3. Vegan cooking. 4. Cookbooks. I. Title. II. Title: One hundred
one globally inspired vegan creations packed with fresh flavors and exciting new tastes. III. Title: One
hundred and one globally inspired vegan creations packed with fresh flavors and exciting new tastes.
 TX838.N485 2011
 641.5'636--dc22

                                                                                    2010049438

Cover and book design: Bradhamdesign.com
Layout: Megan Jones Design
Photography: Celine Steen
Photography on pages 12, 18, 36, 50, 66, 80, 122, 138, 158, 170, 180, 187,
        190, 194, 204, 213, 218: www.thinkstock.com

Printed and bound in China

This book is for Dominic, Nolan, Alayna, and Evelyn; four of the most open-minded little people I know. I love you guys and hope you continue to grow into the beautiful people I know your parents are teaching you to be.

xoxo, Aunt Joni

CONTENTS

FOREWORD

Living vegan makes me appreciate food so much. Good food will leave me talking for days about it, sending photographs to everyone I know, bragging about the latest adventure. I always dream big as to what is possible, what will make the taste buds tingle, and what will leave the tummy full of fuzzies . . . Joni never ceases to dream even bigger with her concoctions, leaving me wide-eyed, amazed, and smiling devilishly. There are things in this cookbook that seem so wild and out there—but end up making perfect sense, and of course, the perfect burger.

It is everything adventurous and it is always extraordinary.

I cherish knowing Joni and her dedication to cooking compassionately, responsibly, and creatively. To be a recipient of her work and her heart leaves me feeling like the luckiest of bears.

—KURT HALSEY FREDERIKSEN,
COMPASSIONATE VEGAN ARTIST FROM PORTLAND, OREGON
WWW.KURTHALSEY.COM

Sunday Afternoon Grillers, page 98

Earth Burger, page 157

Super Quinoa Burger, page 95

Tabbouleh Burger, page 60

INTRODUCTION

You are about to embark on a culinary journey that will test your standard knowledge of ingredients and their form, function, and texture. Foods that you thought should be eaten with a fork or spoon have been transformed into round, handheld patties of goodness that serve up most perfectly between two pieces of bread.

Know this: I have presented you with 101 burgers. But these need not be the limit to your burger concoctions and creations. Be inspired to get into the kitchen and create. Look at those same old ingredients in a whole new way. Anything can become a burger. Anything.

Now, go forth and create a tasty burger!

CHAPTER 1

HOW TO USE THIS BOOK

TiPS, TRiCKS, AND TROUBLESHOOTiNG

Throughout this book you will note that some recipes are listed as soy- or wheat-free. I have taken care to make sure that these recipes do not include the major offenders, but, please, if you have food allergies, or are on a restricted diet, double-check ingredients, especially vinegars, flavor extracts, soy sauces, and other store-bought items.

Look for the following icons as you flip through the book:

WHEAT FREE   **SOY FREE**

You will also notice the use of the terms *sour cream, milk, yogurt, butter, cheese*, and so on. I am sure you already know this, but when mentioned, I mean the nondairy, vegan versions of these ingredients.

One word you will find often in the directions is *dough.* I refer to the mass that forms when you mash all the burger-making ingredients into a patty-able consistency akin to dough. I know this term is usually reserved for baking recipes, but it seems to work efficiently here.

Tips for Reconstituting Textured Vegetable Protein (TVP)

- When microwaving, use plastic wrap to tightly cover your bowl or container. Don't ask me why, but this makes a world of difference, something about how it expands and contracts with the steam.

- If microwaving plastic wrap freaks you out, then you can bring liquid to a boil, pour it over the TVP granules, cover tightly, and let stand for 10 minutes.

- Use 1 cup (235 ml) of liquid per 1 cup (96 g) of TVP when reconstituting, unless otherwise noted.

- Use vegetable broth instead of water for more flavorful TVP.

- You can reconstitute a large batch of TVP all at once, and then store in an airtight container in the fridge. It should keep for up to a week.

Tips for Kneading the "Dough"

- I use my hands. Yes, it's messy, but I find that it gets the job done best. It also ensures that all of the ingredients are well incorporated. In addition, you can feel when the dough is the right consistency. It is easy to tell if you need to add more liquid or dry ingredients using this method.

Tips for Freezing and Refrigerating

- By refrigerating the dough before forming your patties, you are allowing it to stiffen up, making it easier to form. This step is essential when working with gluten-based recipes, because it allows the wheat protein to "rest" and form the stringy texture that helps bind the burgers together.

- To freeze, place the patties in a single layer on a baking sheet. Place in the freezer. Once frozen, pluck 'em off the baking sheet and place in a resealable plastic bag and store in the freezer until needed. Or, place a small sheet of waxed paper between each patty and stack. Place the stack in a resealable plastic bag and store in the freezer until needed.

- There is no need to defrost the patties before cooking. Just plop 'em in a frying pan with a little oil, or bake, grill, or whatever! In fact, it has been my experience, as well as that of a tester or two, that frozen patties cook up better than fresh! They also tend to hold together better.

Tips for Cooking

Most veggie burgers are pretty much already cooked. When you bake, fry, or grill them, you are really just heating them up and giving them a little crust. Here are your options.

BAKING: If you have a Silpat, a silicone baking sheet, or parchment paper, use it! It works better than cooking spray, helps prevent burnt bottoms, and makes cleanup a snap.

When baking, cover your baking sheet or pan with a foil tent (essentially, a steam tent) to help retain moisture.

Most of the burgers can be baked at 350°F (180°C, or gas mark 4) for about 15 minutes per side.

FRYING: I almost exclusively use a cast-iron skillet. That way, I don't have to use too much oil. I preheat the oil in the pan before I add my patties.

I have found that when cooking unfrozen patties, it can take anywhere from 3 to 5 minutes per side over medium-high heat to get a good, golden crispy burger.

I use many types of oil—canola, grapeseed, extra-virgin olive, peanut, sesame— depending on the genre of the burger. Nonstick cooking spray is a good, low-calorie, alternative to oil when frying up a burger. There are other burgers that benefit greatly from a "bake first, then fry" method.

GRILLING: Oil the grill, if possible. This will prevent sticking. Also rub a little oil on both sides of the burger before grilling; it will help you achieve those sought-after grill marks and help prevent sticking.

I like to pick a really hot part of the grill, throw on an oiled frozen patty, let it sit for 3 to 5 minutes on each side, and that's it.

Certain burgers don't hold up that well on the grill, so I use the "steam in foil" method. Loosely wrap the burger in foil and throw it on a not-too-hot portion of the grill and let it steam for 10 to 15 minutes, longer if frozen. You won't get the grill marks, but your burger should remain in one piece. For a little added "juice" you can brush the patty with some olive oil or your favorite flavored oil before steaming on the grill.

ingredients

Some of the ingredients used in this book may be new to you. Here is a short list and brief description of a few key ingredients.

BEANS: Out of laziness, I like to use canned beans, rinsing and draining them thoroughly to get rid of unnecessary extra sodium. If you cook your own, more power to you! Keep in mind that one 15-ounce (425 g) can of beans generally equals approximately 1 ⅔ cups (294 g) cooked beans, or ⅔ cup (120 g) dry beans.

FLOURS: For the sake of accuracy in measurements, I use a scoop to transfer flour into the measuring cup, so as not to over pack it. It can make a difference in how recipes turn out, so it's a good thing to keep in mind. I choose the flour based on the flavor profile of the burger. In general, you can substitute most flours based on what you have on hand, but be sure to pay attention to the consistency of your dough.

LIQUID SMOKE: This flavoring is stocked near the marinades in most markets. It's actually made by condensing smoke into liquid form. A little goes a long way in giving a smoky flavor to many foods.

NONDAIRY MILKS: I most commonly use soymilk, almond milk, or coconut milk when cooking. They seem to have the best results. However, if you have a preference for another type of milk, I am sure it will work just fine. I do recommend using soymilk in recipes when a "buttermilk" texture is needed.

NUTRITIONAL YEAST: This is the magical, nonactive kind of yeast most vegans adore. Its nutty, cheesy flavor makes it an indispensable ingredient in my pantry. Look for the vegetarian-support formula (this will be noted on the label), which is enriched with vitamin B12.

SALT AND PEPPER: I respect your habits when it comes to salt and pepper, so the measurements you will find in my recipes are meant as a guide. I usually add "to taste" so that you can follow your needs and preferences. I prefer using sea salt, because it retains a minuscule amount of minerals. And I like to use a small amount of black salt in recipes that replicate eggs, because it lends a delicate, sulfurous flavor to foods.

SEAWEED, SUCH AS HIJIKI, DULSE, AND NORI: Edible seaweeds add a fishy flavor to foods without using fish.

SOY SAUCE: This condiment can be replaced with tamari or Bragg Liquid Aminos. If you're watchful of your sodium intake, purchase the reduced-sodium kind. The liquid aminos only contain a small amount of natural sodium and happen to be gluten-free.

SRIRACHA OR "ROOSTER SAUCE": Made from chile peppers, garlic, vinegar, and salt ground together to form a smooth paste, this hot sauce is addictive. Check for ingredients, because some brands contain fish sauce.

SUGAR: I do not use refined white sugar. What I commonly refer to as "sugar" is almost always evaporated cane juice. Most refined white sugar is processed using charred animal bones. I prefer to keep the bones out of my sugar, so I stick with the more natural, cruelty-free versions.

TEMPEH: Tempeh is made from fermented soybeans pressed into a cake. Bitter to some, this whole-bean soy treat is a very versatile protein. Still afraid? Simmer tempeh in water or vegetable broth for about 20 minutes prior to using in recipes. It mellows the flavor.

VITAL WHEAT GLUTEN FLOUR: Gluten is the natural protein portion removed from whole wheat. Vital wheat gluten flour can be found in most grocery stores or ordered online. It is important to know that vital wheat gluten flour is completely different from high gluten flour. The two are not interchangeable and will not perform similarly in recipes.

CHAPTER 2

BURGERS FOR BREAKFAST

CAN YOU THINK OF A BETTER WAY TO START YOUR DAY?

1. Denver Omelet Burger
2. Bacon and Egg Breakfast Burger
3. Garlicky Ranch Potato Burger
4. Chicken Fried Steak Burger
5. Log Cabin Burger
6. O'Brien Burger
7. Sweet Caramelized Onion Burger
8. Peaches and Cream Burger
9. PB & J Burger
10. Cherry Oatmeal Protein-Packed Energy Burger

Denver Omelet Burger

This just might be my favorite burger in the entire book! It makes such a great, hearty breakfast with all the flavors you remember and love from a traditional Denver Omelet.

INGREDIENTS:

12 ounces (340 g) extra-firm tofu, drained and pressed

½ cup (120 ml) plus 2 tablespoons (30 ml) canola or other vegetable oil, divided, plus more for frying

1 teaspoon garlic powder

1 teaspoon onion powder

1 teaspoon mustard powder

½ teaspoon cumin

¼ teaspoon turmeric

¼ teaspoon paprika

1 cup (160 g) diced onion

1 red bell pepper, cored, seeded, and diced

1 green bell pepper, cored, seeded, and diced

⅛ teaspoon salt

¼ cup (25 g) imitation bacon bits, store-bought or homemade (page 185)

¼ cup (40 g) diced "Ham" (page 117, optional)

½ teaspoon liquid smoke

1 cup (120 g) chickpea (garbanzo) flour

DIRECTIONS:

In a blender, combine the tofu, ½ cup (120 ml) oil, garlic powder, onion powder, mustard powder, cumin, turmeric, and paprika, and process until smooth. Transfer to a mixing bowl and set aside.

Preheat the 2 tablespoons (30 ml) oil in a frying pan. Add the onion, bell peppers, and salt. Sauté until just beginning to brown. Remove from the heat and add to the tofu mixture.

Fold in the bacon bits, "Ham," and liquid smoke.

Add the chickpea flour and mix. The mixture is wet and sticky, but you should be able to form it into 6 patties.

Preheat plenty of oil in a frying pan and panfry for about 5 minutes per side, or until golden and crispy.

YiELD: 6 BURGERS

SERVING SUGGESTION

Serve up warm topped with some salsa or nondairy sour cream (page 191) on a toasted English muffin or bagel with some home fries or hash browns.

Bacon and Egg Breakfast Burger

2

Fake bacon and tofu eggs go together like peanut butter and jelly in this burger than knocks the socks off any fast food breakfast sammy.

INGREDIENTS:

12 ounces (340 g) extra-firm tofu, drained and pressed

¼ teaspoon turmeric

1 tablespoon (8 g) garlic powder

1 tablespoon (8 g) onion powder

1 tablespoon (15 g) yellow mustard

¼ teaspoon sea salt

¼ cup (25 g) imitation bacon bits, store-bought or homemade (page 185)

½ to 1 cup (62 to 125 g) all-purpose flour

2 tablespoons (30 ml) oil, for frying

DIRECTIONS:

Crumble the tofu into a large mixing bowl.

Add the turmeric, garlic powder, onion powder, mustard, salt, and bacon bits, and stir to combine.

Knead in the flour a little at a time. Depending on how much moisture was left in your tofu, you may need a little or a lot. Knead the heck out of this until you get a nice ball of dough, at least 5 minutes.

Let sit for at least 15 minutes to rest. Divide the dough into 4 equal parts and form into patties. Panfry in the oil for 4 to 5 minutes per side, or until nice and golden brown.

YIELD: 4 BURGERS

SERVING SUGGESTION

When you're on the go, eat this on a whole wheat bun, an English muffin, or Bagel Bun (page 202), with a slice of vegan cheese or a little vegan garlic mayo. At home you can add a side of hash browns or home fries. Garnish with your favorite breakfast toppings (think omelet here: diced and grilled peppers and onions, salsa, Smart Bacon, ketchup, avocado, or spinach).

Garlicky Ranch Potato Burger

SOY FREE

These are carb-o-licious. If you are looking for a low-carb or low-cal burger, then don't make these. They work well for breakfast, lunch, or dinner. Furthermore, they don't even need a bun!

INGREDIENTS:

2 cups (220 g) shredded potatoes (tightly packed), rinsed in cool water and drained to prevent discoloring

2 tablespoons (30 g) minced garlic

1 tablespoon (2 g) dried parsley or 3 tablespoons (12 g) chopped fresh parsley

1 teaspoon paprika

Salt and pepper

1 cup (115 g) panko bread crumbs

½ cup (62 g) all-purpose flour

2 tablespoons (13 g) ground flaxseed mixed with 3 tablespoons (45 ml) water

⅓ cup (80 ml) canola oil, plus extra for frying

DIRECTIONS:

In a large bowl, combine the potatoes, garlic, parsley, paprika, and salt and pepper to taste. Mix until all of the potatoes are well coated.

Add the panko, flour, flax mixture, and ⅓ cup (80 ml) oil.

Mix well, using your hands, until a nice dough forms. Divide into 4 to 6 equal pieces and form into patties. The thinner your patty, the crispier it will be.

Preheat a generous amount of oil in a skillet and panfry for 3 to 5 minutes per side, or until golden and crispy.

YIELD: 4 TO 6 BURGERS

SERVING SUGGESTION

No bun needed, just a schmear of good old-fashioned ketchup. If you're having them for breakfast, serve with a nice tofu scramble. For lunch or dinner, serve with a nice green vegetable to balance out the carb overload. Or just go crazy and serve with a nice side of Garlicky Roasted Reds (see note at right) and run a marathon the next day.

RECIPE NOTE

To make Garlicky Roasted Reds to serve alongside these burgers, first cut up a bag of baby red potatoes into bite-size chunks. Spread them in a single layer on a foil-lined baking sheet, with the skins down, and sprinkle with salt, pepper, paprika, garlic powder, parsley, and fresh minced garlic. Then drizzle a bit of olive oil over the whole thing and bake at 350°F (180°C, or gas mark 4) for about 30 minutes.

Chicken Fried Steak Burger

Greasy breakfasts are my number one way to cure an aching belly after a night of too much fun. They're also one of my favorite ways to make dinner!

FOR PATTiES:

1 pound (454 g) prepared seitan, store-bought or homemade (page 217)

½ cup (62 g) all-purpose flour

¼ cup (60 ml) vegetable oil

1 tablespoon (2 g) dried parsley or 3 tablespoons (12 g) chopped fresh parsley

Salt and pepper

Oil, for frying

FOR BREADiNG:

1 cup (125 g) all-purpose flour

¼ cup (30 g) nutritional yeast

1 teaspoon paprika

Salt and pepper

1 cup (235 ml) nondairy milk

DiRECTiONS:

To make the patties: Combine all the ingredients in a food processor and process until a dough ball forms. If your mixture is too dry, add in a little more oil, 1 teaspoon (5 ml) at a time. If it is too wet, add in a little more flour, 1 tablespoon (8 g) at a time.

Divide the dough into 4 equal pieces and form into patties. Set aside.

Preheat a skillet with plenty of oil.

To make the breading: Mix together all the ingredients except milk and place in a shallow dish.

Place the milk in a shallow dish.

Dip each patty into the milk, then dredge in the flour mixture, then dip into the milk again, and then dredge in the flour mixture again. This is known as "double dredging."

Fry each patty for approximately 5 minutes per side, or until very golden brown and crispy.

YiELD: 4 BURGERS

SERViNG SUGGESTiON

Serve open-faced on Simple Biscuits (page 198) topped with your favorite gravy.

Log Cabin Burger

The marriage of sweet and savory was the inspiration for this burger. This is my idea of a pancake mixed together with a sausage, all in one little package.

INGREDIENTS:

8 ounces (225 g) plain soy tempeh

1 cup (125 g) all-purpose flour

⅓ cup (80 ml) pure maple syrup

¼ cup (56 g) nondairy butter

2 tablespoons (32 g) peanut butter

1 tablespoon (8 g) vegetable broth powder or ½ bouillon cube, crumbled

1 teaspoon liquid smoke

⅛ teaspoon paprika

Salt and pepper

Oil, for frying (optional)

DIRECTIONS:

In a mixing bowl, crumble the tempeh into the smallest bits possible. Add the flour, maple syrup, butter, peanut butter, vegetable broth powder, liquid smoke, paprika, and salt and pepper to taste. Mix well, using your hands, until a nice dough forms.

Divide into 4 equal pieces and form into patties.

Cook as desired. Bake at 350°F (180°C, or gas mark 4) for 30 minutes, covered loosely in foil, flipping halfway through, or panfry in a small amount of oil over medium-high heat for 3 to 4 minutes per side.

YIELD: 4 BURGERS

SERVING SUGGESTION

To pull out the savory flavors, add a dollop of ketchup and eat it on its own, or sandwich the burger inside a homemade Bagel Bun (page 202) or Rustica Bun (page 199). To pull out the sweet flavors, serve on its own topped with a dollop of nondairy butter and some pure maple syrup. Served with a nice tofu scramble, this makes a very hearty breakfast.

6 O'Brien Burger WHEAT FREE

Potatoes O'Brien are an Irish breakfast treat. Bright, colorful, and crunchy peppers give this patty a great texture. Enjoy this twist on a classic for breakfast, lunch, or dinner!

INGREDIENTS:

3 cups (330 g) shredded russet potatoes, rinsed in cool water and drained to prevent discoloring

1 yellow onion, diced

1 green bell pepper, cored, seeded, and diced

1 cup (240 g) nondairy sour cream, store-bought or homemade (page 191)

¼ cup (113 g) diced pimiento

Salt and pepper

3 cups (360 g) chickpea flour

Oil, for frying

DIRECTIONS:

In a large mixing bowl, combine the potatoes, onion, bell pepper, sour cream, pimiento, and salt and pepper to taste. Slowly add the chickpea flour and mix until well incorporated. The mixture should be very wet.

Form into 8 patties. Line a plate with paper towels.

Preheat ¼ inch (6 mm) oil in a large frying pan over high heat. The oil is ready when a piece of dough dropped into it sizzles immediately.

Fry each patty for 3 to 5 minutes per side, or until extra golden and crispy.

Transfer to the plate to drain the excess oil.

YIELD: 8 BURGERS

SERVING SUGGESTION

Serve on a toasted bun with a schmear of vegan mayo, crisp lettuce, a nice slice of juicy tomato, and some ripe avocado.

Sweet Caramelized Onion Burger

WHEAT FREE **SOY FREE**

Sometimes sweet and savory with a bit of salty is all I crave. This burger fits the bill perfectly, especially for breakfast.

INGREDIENTS:

2 tablespoons (30 ml) vegetable oil, plus more for frying (optional)

1 large white onion, julienned

5 ounces (140 g) mushrooms, chopped or sliced

2 tablespoons (30 g) minced garlic

Sea salt and pepper

2 tablespoons (30 ml) pure maple syrup

2 tablespoons (30 ml) balsamic vinegar

1 cup (160 g) rice flour

2 tablespoons (16 g) cornstarch

¼ cup (30 g) pine nuts

1 tablespoon (2 g) dried parsley

¼ teaspoon liquid smoke (optional)

SERVING SUGGESTION

For a hearty breakfast, serve this burger with some fresh asparagus spears and garlic smashed or home fried potatoes on the side.

DIRECTIONS:

Preheat the 2 tablespoons (30 ml) oil in a skillet over medium-high heat. Add the onion, mushrooms, and garlic. Add a pinch of sea salt to really get those onions sweating. Sauté, turning often, until the mushrooms have reduced in size by about half, or about 5 minutes.

Add the maple syrup and vinegar, lower the heat to medium, and cook for about 10 minutes longer, stirring occasionally, or until most of the liquid has been absorbed. Add a liberal amount of freshly cracked pepper to taste. Remove from the heat and let cool.

Transfer to a mixing bowl. Add the flour, cornstarch, pine nuts, parsley, and liquid smoke, and knead until a nice dough forms. If you think the mixture feels too dry, don't worry; keep kneading and it will come together, I promise.

Form into 4 patties.

Cook as desired. Bake at 350°F (180°C, or gas mark 4) for 30 minutes on a baking sheet lined with parchment or a silicone baking mat, covered loosely in foil, flipping halfway through. Or panfry in a small amount of oil over medium-high heat for about 3 minutes per side, or until a nice crispy crust forms.

YIELD: 4 BURGERS

8 Peaches and Cream Burger

Okay, this one is really more like a cross between a thick pancake and a sweet biscuit than it is a true burger, but it's yummy and that's really what counts, right?

FOR TOPPING:

8 ounces (225 g) sliced frozen, canned, or fresh peaches, skins removed

1 cup (235 ml) soy creamer

⅓ cup (67 g) sugar

¼ cup (56 g) nondairy butter

1 tablespoon (8 g) cornstarch dissolved in ¼ cup (60 ml) water to make a slurry

½ cup (120 g) nondairy sour cream, store-bought or homemade (page 191)

1 teaspoon vanilla extract

FOR BURGERS:

2 cups (250 g) all-purpose flour

¼ cup (50 g) sugar

½ teaspoon baking soda

½ teaspoon baking powder

¼ teaspoon salt

1 cup (235 ml) soy or other nondairy milk

1 container (6 ounces, or 170 g) vanilla-flavored nondairy yogurt

1 teaspoon pure vanilla extract

DIRECTIONS:

To make the topping: In a pot, combine the peaches, creamer, sugar, and butter. Bring to a boil, and reduce to a simmer. Simmer for about 15 minutes. The peaches should be soft and beginning to fall apart.

Add the cornstarch slurry, stir, and remove from the heat. Stir in the sour cream and vanilla. Stir until smooth and creamy. Keep warm until ready to serve.

To make the burgers: In a mixing bowl, whisk together the flour, sugar, baking soda, baking powder, and salt.

In a separate bowl, combine the milk, yogurt, and vanilla.

Add the dry ingredients to the wet and stir to combine. Your mixture will be thick, not runny.

Preheat a flat, nonstick skillet over high heat. Drop about ½ cup (115 g) of the mixture onto the hot, dry pan and let cook for about 3 minutes. You need to let them cook longer than traditional pancakes due to their thickness, but be careful not to burn. Flip and cook an additional 3 minutes. Repeat to make 6 burgers.

YIELD: 6 BURGERS

SERVING SUGGESTION

Serve hot, topped with the warm peach topping and some fresh raspberries. Add a side of nondairy yogurt for a complete meal.

PB & J Burger

SOY FREE

What could be better than super simple ingredients and a super simple recipe. Go ahead. Call them cookies. I call them breakfast!

INGREDIENTS:

1 cup (256 g) creamy no-stir peanut butter

1 cup (320 g) your favorite jelly or jam

2 cups (250 g) all-purpose flour

½ teaspoon baking soda

½ teaspoon baking powder

⅛ teaspoon salt

DIRECTIONS:

Preheat the oven to 350°F (180°C, or gas mark 4). Line a baking sheet with parchment or a silicone baking mat.

In a mixing bowl, combine all the ingredients and knead until a soft, shiny dough forms. Depending on the amount of oil/moisture in your peanut butter, you may need to adjust the amount of flour.

Form into 8 patties. Place on the prepared baking sheet.

Bake for 15 to 20 minutes, or until the tops are nice and crackly.

YIELD: 8 BURGERS (COOKIES!)

SERVING SUGGESTION

All alone is fine, but I like them warm, right out of the oven, with a schmear of nondairy cream cheese and extra jam!

10 Cherry Oatmeal Protein-Packed Energy Burger

I need something to take with me on my 45-minute drive to work at 4:00 a.m., because I simply refuse to get up even one minute earlier than I need to. These work nicely. They are ultra portable and keep me satisfied all the way 'til lunchtime.

INGREDIENTS:

½ cup (80 g) rice flour

½ cup (56 g) coconut flour

1 cup (80 g) quick-cooking oats

1 cup (120 g) dried cherries or your favorite dried fruit

½ cup (92 g) soy protein powder

½ cup (110 g) firmly packed brown sugar

½ cup (65 g) raw cashews or your nut of choice

¼ cup (29 g) wheat germ

¼ cup (32 g) hulled pumpkin seeds

¼ cup (32 g) hulled sunflower seeds

½ teaspoon baking powder

½ teaspoon baking soda

½ teaspoon sea salt

½ teaspoon ground cinnamon

1 container (6 ounces, or 170 g) vanilla-flavored nondairy yogurt

½ cup (120 ml) nondairy milk

¼ cup (64 g) cashew nut butter

¼ cup (84 g) agave nectar

¼ cup (60 ml melted or 56 g solid) coconut oil

DIRECTIONS:

Preheat the oven to 350°F (180°C, or gas mark 4). Line a baking sheet with parchment or a silicone baking mat.

In a large mixing bowl, combine the flours, oats, dried cherries, protein powder, brown sugar, cashews, wheat germ, pumpkin seeds, sunflower seeds, baking powder, baking soda, salt, and cinnamon.

In a separate bowl, whisk together the yogurt, milk, nut butter, agave, and coconut oil.

Add the dry ingredients to the wet and mix well, using your hands, until a nice dough forms.

Divide into 8 portions. Form into patties. Place on the prepared baking sheet.

Bake, uncovered, for 18 to 20 minutes, or until the tops just start to crack.

YIELD: 8 BURGERS

SERVING SUGGESTION

Serve with a tall cup of coffee (or soy milk), of course!

CHAPTER 3

BURGERS FROM THE FAR EAST

INSPIRED BY THE FLAVORS OF ASIA

11 Thai-inspired Black Bean Tofu and Potato Patties

These are really spicy, but you can cool them down a bit by reducing the red pepper flakes by half without changing the intended flavor. Me? I like 'em spicy.

INGREDIENTS:

4 red potatoes (about 1 ¼ pounds [193 g])

12 ounces (340 g) extra-firm tofu, drained and pressed

1 can (15 ounces, or 420 g) black beans, drained and rinsed

¼ cup (64 g) peanut butter

½ cup (48 g) finely chopped scallions

2 tablespoons (30 g) dried red pepper flakes

2 tablespoons (30 g) minced garlic

1 teaspoon green curry paste

1 teaspoon Sriracha sauce

¼ teaspoon dried ground coriander

Salt and pepper

¼ cup (30 g) whole wheat pastry flour

SERVING SUGGESTION

Tuck it into a whole wheat bun on a bed of shredded cabbage and slather with Thai Peanut Sauce (page 193). Serve with a side of Thai-style peanut coleslaw.

DIRECTIONS:

Preheat the oven to 350°F (180°C, or gas mark 4). Have ready a nonstick baking sheet.

Bring a pot of salted water to a boil.

Cut the potatoes into approximately 1-inch (2.5 cm) chunks, leaving the skin on. Place the potatoes in the boiling water and let boil for 10 to 12 minutes, or until fork-tender. Drain and set aside to cool.

Meanwhile, crumble the tofu into a mixing bowl, and add the beans, peanut butter, scallions, red pepper flakes, garlic, curry paste, Sriracha sauce, coriander, and salt and pepper to taste.

When the potatoes are cool enough to handle, add them to the tofu mixture, and knead together with your hands until everything is well combined.

Depending on the moistness of your mix, add more or less of the ¼ cup (30 g) flour. Form into 10 patties, place on the baking sheet, and cover with foil. Bake for 15 minutes per side, or until crispy.

YIELD: 10 BURGERS

Chinese Take-Out Burger

This burger is super fun to make and the additions and substitutions you can make are only limited by your imagination. Here is the basic recipe with suggestions for optional add-ins. I use white rice for a base because sticky white rice is what I think of when I think of Chinese take-out. However, you can use brown rice instead. Serve up alongside some stir-fried bok choy or crispy noodles.

FOR GLAZE:

1½ cups (355 ml) water

2 tablespoons (30 ml) orange juice

¼ cup (60 ml) lemon juice

⅓ cup (80 ml) rice vinegar (in a pinch you can use 2 tablespoons [30 ml] apple cider vinegar)

2½ tablespoons (38 ml) soy sauce

1 tablespoon (6 g) grated orange zest or 1 teaspoon orange extract

1 cup (225 g) firmly packed brown sugar

½ teaspoon freshly minced gingerroot or ¼ teaspoon ground

1 teaspoon minced garlic

½ teaspoon red pepper flakes

3 tablespoons (24 g) cornstarch dissolved in 2 tablespoons (30 ml) water to make a slurry

FOR PATTIES:

2 cups (348 g) fully cooked white rice (you can use any rice you want to, really!)

8 ounces (227 g) plain soy tempeh, crumbled almost into individual beans

½ cup (60 g) chickpea flour (you can probably use plain old all-purpose here too, but I like the flavor of the chickpea flour)

1 tablespoon (6 g) orange zest or 1 teaspoon orange extract

Add-ins (optional): peas, grated carrots, chopped broccoli, diced red peppers, soy sauce, chopped scallions (you know, the stuff you would find in Chinese take-out fried rice)!

FOR COATING:

1 cup (120 g) chickpea flour

½ cup (120 ml) nondairy milk

1 cup (115 g) panko bread crumbs

Oil, for frying

DIRECTIONS:

To make the glaze: Combine all the glaze ingredients, except for the cornstarch slurry, in a saucepan and bring to a boil, stirring occasionally. Reduce to a simmer and slowly add the cornstarch mixture; continue to stir as it thickens. Lower the heat to keep warm and reserve.

To make the patties: Mix together all the ingredients, using your hands. Squeeze and knead until it becomes very sticky. Form into 5 or 6 patties.

To make the coating: Combine the flour and milk in a bowl. Spread the bread crumbs on a shallow plate. Heat the oil in a frying pan over medium-high heat.

Coat each patty with the flour and milk mixture, and then dredge in the bread crumbs. Place in the frying pan and fry until golden and crispy on each side, 3 to 5 minutes per side. Remove from the oil and dip into the glaze to generously coat both sides.

YIELD: 5 OR 6 BURGERS

Chow Mein Burger

You can add all kinds of veggies to this one. I stuck with carrots and broccoli, but baby corn, edamame, red bell peppers, mung bean sprouts, sugar snap peas, or whatever else you have on hand would make a great addition to the recipe.

INGREDIENTS:

1 package (6 ounces, or 170 g) chow mein noodles

2 tablespoons (30 ml) sesame oil

8 ounces (227 g) broccoli florets

1 cup (108 g) sliced or shredded carrots

½ cup (65 g) raw cashew pieces

1 tablespoon (6 g) grated fresh ginger

2 tablespoons (30 ml) peanut oil

12 ounces (340 g) extra-firm tofu, drained, pressed, and cut into small cubes

¼ cup (60 ml) soy sauce or tamari

1 tablespoon (8 g) sesame seeds

½ cup (128 g) cashew nut butter

¼ cup (32 g) potato starch or cornstarch

Salt and pepper

Oil, for frying

SERVING SUGGESTION

Serve piping hot, topped with extra chow mein noodles and sprinkled with a few sesame seeds over a bed of steamed cabbage with a dollop of Chinese hot mustard, hot ketchup, or Sriracha for dipping.

DIRECTIONS:

Prepare the noodles according to the package instructions. Drain, divide, into two equal portions, and set aside.

Using a wok or a large frying pan, heat the sesame oil. Add the broccoli, carrots, cashew pieces, and ginger. Stir-fry for 5 to 7 minutes.

Add the peanut oil, then the tofu. Continue to cook 5 more minutes, tossing often.

Add the soy sauce, half of the noodles, and the sesame seeds. Toss to coat and continue to cook 5 minutes longer.

Turn off the heat and add the cashew butter, stirring to coat. Let cool.

Sprinkle in the potato starch and, using your hands, knead together. Season with salt and pepper.

Form into 6 patties. Line a plate with paper towels.

Preheat ¼ inch (6 mm) oil in a frying pan over high heat. The oil is ready when a piece of dough dropped into it sizzles immediately.

Fry the patties for about 5 minutes per side, until a nice crispy, golden brown crust forms. Transfer to the plate to drain excess oil.

Serve with the remaining half of the chow mein noodles.

YIELD: 6 BURGERS

14 Sweet and Sour Pork Mini Burger

This sauce here also tastes great tossed with your favorite veggie protein and served over rice and steamed veggies.

FOR SAUCE:

¾ cup (180 ml) pineapple juice

¼ cup (50 g) sugar

2 tablespoons (34 g) ketchup

2 tablespoons (30 ml) soy sauce

1 teaspoon red pepper flakes

¼ cup (60 ml) rice wine vinegar

1 tablespoon (8 g) cornstarch dissolved in ¼ cup (60 ml) water to make a slurry

FOR BURGERS:

Oil, for frying

½ cup (120 ml) soymilk

½ cup (62 g) all-purpose flour

¼ cup (32 g) cornstarch

1 recipe "Ham" (page 117)

DIRECTIONS:

To make the sauce: In a saucepan, combine the pineapple juice, sugar, ketchup, soy sauce, and red pepper flakes. Bring to a boil. Stir in the vinegar. Turn off the heat and stir in the cornstarch slurry. Stir until thickened. Keep warm over very low heat until the burgers are ready to coat.

Preheat ¼ inch (6 mm) of oil in a frying pan over high heat. The oil is ready when a piece of dough dropped into it sizzles immediately.

Pour the soymilk into a shallow dish. In another shallow dish, combine the flour and cornstarch.

Slice the "ham" into twelve ¼-inch (6 mm)-thick slices. Dip each slice into the soymilk, and then dredge in the flour mixture.

Fry for 2 to 3 minutes per side, or until crispy and golden brown.

Transfer directly to the sauce and turn to coat.

YIELD: 12 MINI BURGERS

SERVING SUGGESTION

Serve on a plain white bun (page 196) with crunchy shredded cabbage. Add a side of stir-fried veggies and sticky rice to round out the meal.

Three Pepper Stir-Fry Burger

WHEAT FREE **SOY FREE**

15

If you have a wok, this is a good time to use it. If not, use your largest frying pan or even a stockpot.

INGREDIENTS:

2 tablespoons (30 ml) oil

2 cups (320 g) diced red onion

8 ounces (227 g) mushrooms, chopped

1 red bell pepper, cored, seeded, and diced

1 yellow bell pepper, cored, seeded, and diced

1 green bell pepper, cored, seeded, and diced

3 cups (522 g) cooked brown rice

2 tablespoons (32 g) peanut butter

3 tablespoons (45 ml) sesame oil

1 teaspoon cumin

1 tablespoon (17 g) Sriracha sauce

3 tablespoons (24 g) arrowroot powder

SERVING SUGGESTION

I like to serve these up bun-less on a nice big leaf of purple cabbage with some Thai Peanut Sauce (page 193).

DIRECTIONS:

Preheat a wok, add the oil to heat, then add the onion, mushrooms, and bell peppers. Stir-fry over high heat for about 10 minutes, stirring often, until the vegetables have reduced in volume by about half. Remove from the heat.

Stir in the rice, peanut butter, sesame oil, cumin, Sriracha, and arrowroot powder. Mix well.

Refrigerate for at least 20 minutes to thicken up a bit. You can refrigerate overnight, if desired.

Preheat the oven to 350°F (180°C, or gas mark 4). Line a baking sheet with parchment or a silicone baking mat, or spray with nonstick spray.

Form the mixture into 8 patties and place on the prepared baking sheet.

Bake, uncovered, for 15 to 20 minutes, then gently flip and bake 15 to 20 minutes longer, until firm and just beginning to brown. Remove from the oven and let sit for about 10 minutes before serving.

YIELD: 8 BURGERS

16 Beef and Broccoli Burger

These are like a bowl from one of those take-out joints, but in the shape of a burger! A caveat: I make these ones really big and really, really chunky. I like 'em that way. You can certainly improve the stability of your burgers, especially if you want to serve them on a bun, by simply placing all of the ingredients in a food processor and pulsing a few times before forming into patties.

INGREDIENTS:

1 pound (454 g) prepared seitan, store-bought or homemade (page 217), chopped into small pieces

8 ounces (227 g) broccoli florets, chopped to the size of your liking

2 cups (348 g) cooked sushi or plain white rice

½ cup (62 g) all-purpose or ½ cup (80 g) rice flour

½ cup (120 ml) teriyaki sauce

1 tablespoon (15 ml) rice vinegar

1 tablespoon (8 g) sesame seeds

DIRECTIONS:

In a mixing bowl, combine the seitan, broccoli, rice, and flour. Knead to combine. This is a very sticky mixture.

Form into 4 to 6 patties and set aside.

Whisk together the teriyaki sauce, vinegar, and sesame seeds. Pour into a large nonstick pan and bring to a simmer.

Place the patties in the pan, simmer for 5 to 7 minutes, flip and cook 5 minutes longer. The patties will absorb most, if not all, of the liquid.

YIELD: 4 GIANT BURGERS OR 6 HUMAN-SIZE ONES

SERVING SUGGESTION

I don't think these need a bun. I like to serve mine with the typical take-out-style sides.

Moo Goo Gai Pan Burger

WHEAT FREE

This burger is full of exotic flavor and ingredients. It creates quite a delightful aroma when you make it, so don't be surprised when everyone in the house wanders into the kitchen while you're cooking!

INGREDIENTS:

2 tablespoons (30 ml) sesame oil

8 ounces (227 g) sliced mushrooms

5 ounces (140 g) sliced bamboo shoots

5 ounces (140 g) sliced water chestnuts

3½ tablespoons (28 g) chopped or grated fresh ginger

2 tablespoons (30 g) minced garlic

Salt and pepper

⅔ cup (160 ml) soy sauce

⅓ cup (80 ml) rice wine vinegar

2 tablespoons (16 g) cornstarch dissolved in ¼ cup (60 ml) water to make a slurry

4 cups (700 g) cooked sushi rice

1 cup (160 g) white rice flour

¼ cup (64 g) tahini paste

Oil, for frying (optional)

DIRECTIONS:

Preheat a wok or large frying pan, then add the sesame oil and heat. Add the mushrooms, bamboo shoots, water chestnuts, ginger, and garlic. Add a pinch of salt. Sauté until the mushrooms have reduced in size by about half, 7 to 10 minutes.

Add the soy sauce and vinegar, bring to a boil, slowly add the cornstarch slurry, and remove from the heat.

Add the rice, rice flour, tahini, and salt and pepper to taste and mix well. Let rest for about 20 minutes. The mixture will be sticky.

Meanwhile, preheat the oven to 350°F (180°C, or gas mark 4). Line a baking sheet with parchment or a silicone baking mat.

Form the mixture into 8 patties and place on the prepared baking sheet.

Bake, covered in foil, for 30 minutes, flipping halfway through.

For an extra-crispy crust, panfry in a bit of oil for 2 to 3 minutes per side, after baking.

YIELD: 8 BURGERS

SERVING SUGGESTION

I like these served solo on a bed of cabbage (steamed or raw) topped with a dollop of spicy Chinese mustard and hot ketchup. On the side? Sticky or fried rice.

18 Edamame Burger

WHEAT FREE

Yep, green burgers. This recipe makes a lot, but they freeze well, so you can have green burgers all week long!

INGREDIENTS:

2 cups (340 g) shelled and frozen edamame

1 can (15 ounces, or 420 g) chickpeas, with liquid

8 ounces (227 g) sliced mushrooms

½ cup (65 g) finely ground raw cashews

½ cup (60 g) nutritional yeast

4 cloves garlic

½ teaspoon ground cumin

¼ teaspoon liquid smoke (optional)

1 teaspoon Bragg's Liquid Aminos or soy sauce

Salt and pepper, to taste

3½ cups (420 g) chickpea flour

Oil, for frying

DIRECTIONS:

Place the frozen edamame and the entire can of chickpeas, including the liquid, in a saucepot and warm through. This step is to defrost the edamame; if you use fresh or precooked edamame, you can skip this step.

Combine the edamame, chickpeas and liquid, mushrooms, cashews, yeast, garlic, cumin, liquid smoke, liquid aminos, and salt and pepper in a food processor and process until smooth. Pour into a large bowl.

Slowly add the flour until a thicker consistency is formed. Depending on the moisture content of your mixture, you may need just a little flour or a whole lot.

Place the entire bowl in the refrigerator for 20 to 30 minutes to stiffen up and make it easier to handle when forming the patties. Form into 16 patties.

Heat the oil in a sauté pan and fry the patties for 4 to 5 minutes, or until golden brown on both sides.

YIELD: 16 BURGERS

SERVING SUGGESTION

Serve bunless with a side of Sweet Potato Fries (page 206, and pictured here) and Chipotle Dipping Sauce (page 184, and pictured here); or, serve on a soft white roll with the traditional burger fixin's.

19 Wasabi Burger

Not necessarily intended to taste like sushi, these have a touch of that wasabi spice paired with the sweet taste of nori to create a sensation of yum!

INGREDIENTS:

½ cup (120 g) nondairy cream cheese

2 tablespoons (30 ml) rice vinegar

2 teaspoons (3 g) wasabi powder

2 tablespoons (36 g) white miso

3 cups (522 g) cooked sushi rice

3 nori sheets, torn into tiny pieces

1 cup (115 g) panko bread crumbs

Oil, for frying

DIRECTIONS:

In a mixing bowl, combine the cream cheese, vinegar, wasabi powder, and miso until nice and creamy.

Mix in the rice, nori pieces, and panko.

Using your hands, squish together the mixture until all the ingredients are well incorporated. The mixture will be sticky. Form into 6 to 8 patties.

Preheat a skillet with oil and panfry for 3 to 5 minutes per side, or until a nice golden brown crust forms.

YIELD: 6 TO 8 BURGERS

SERVING SUGGESTION

I like to serve these with a couple of fried wonton wrappers to give it a bit of crunch. A nice side dish would be some miso soup and a bowl of edamame.

RECIPE NOTE

Not a fan of wasabi? Substitute Chinese hot mustard for the wasabi powder.

Korean BBQ Burger

Spicy with a hint of sweet, these burgers were inspired by some Korean spicy fries that I got off a food truck in Long Beach, California—so good!

INGREDIENTS:

1 tablespoon (15 ml) sesame oil

1 to 3 tablespoons (15 to 45 g) chili garlic sauce or Sambal Oelek

4 cloves garlic, minced

1 cup (57 g) instant potato flakes

1 can (15 ounces, or 420 g) white beans, drained and rinsed

2 tablespoons (12 g) finely chopped scallion or chives

½ cup (65 g) raw cashews, finely ground into a powder

2 tablespoons (42 g) agave nectar

2 tablespoons (16 g) cornstarch

3 tablespoons (45 ml) canola oil

Salt and pepper

Oil, for frying (optional)

DIRECTIONS:

Add all the ingredients to a mixing bowl, and mash together using your hands. Really smoosh it together until there are almost no whole beans left in the mixture. Let rest for at least 20 minutes to thicken up a bit.

Form into 4 patties.

Panfry in oil over medium-high heat for 2 to 3 minutes per side, or until a golden, crispy crust is formed, or bake, uncovered, on a baking sheet lined with parchment or a silicone baking mat at 350°F (180°C, or gas mark 4) for 25 minutes, or until firm and just beginning to brown.

YIELD: 4 BURGERS

SERVING SUGGESTION

If soy and wheat are not issues for you, I suggest serving these on a soft white bun, lightly toasted and schmeared with nondairy cream cheese mixed with a little bit of Sriracha sauce.

CHAPTER 4

BURGERS FROM THE MIDDLE EAST

FILLED WITH THE EXOTIC FLAVORS AND AROMAS OF THE REGION

Baba Ghanoush Burger

WHEAT FREE

Baba ghanoush is traditionally a paste made from eggplant, garlic, cumin, and spices. It is traditionally used as a spread or dip with flatbreads or crackers. In some countries, cooks add onions and tahini to the mix. For this recipe, I incorporated them right into the burger.

INGREDIENTS:

2 tablespoons (30 ml) sesame oil

12 ounces (340 g) peeled and cubed eggplant

2 tablespoons (30 g) minced garlic

8 ounces (227 g) diced onion

1 teaspoon cumin

Salt and pepper

½ cup (120 ml) vegetable broth

¾ cup (72 g) TVP granules

1 cup (120 g) chickpea flour

Oil, for frying (optional)

SERVING SUGGESTION

This burger would be perfect on flatbread or in a pita. Hummus makes a nice spread, as does the Garlic Artichoke Spread (page 188). A nice side dish would be traditional Tabbouleh Salad (page 60), as as shown here.

DIRECTIONS:

Preheat the sesame oil in a skillet over medium-high heat. Add the eggplant, cook for about 5 minutes.

Add the garlic, diced onion, cumin, and salt and pepper to taste. Cook for 15 minutes, uncovered, turning occasionally.

Add the vegetable broth, then stir in the TVP. Cover and remove from the heat. Let stand for at least 10 minutes.

Uncover and stir in the flour. Mix very well.

Cover and refrigerate for at least 30 minutes, or even until the next day. The longer you leave it in the fridge, the more the flour will absorb the flavors of the mixture. In addition, refrigeration helps make the patties easier to form.

Preheat the oven to 350°F (180°C, or gas mark 4).

Form into 4 to 6 patties. Bake, uncovered, for 20 minutes, or until firm and just beginning to brown. Then, if desired, fry in oil for 2 to 3 minutes per side, until a nice golden crust forms.

YIELD: 4 TO 6 BURGERS

22 Curried Split Pea Burger

Other than the cooking of the peas, these tasty burgers come together quickly and easily. If you are really into curry, the way I am, feel free to double the amount listed in the recipe.

INGREDIENTS:

3 cups (705 ml) lightly salted water

1 cup (225 g) dried split peas

3 tablespoons (45 ml) sesame oil

1 tablespoon (6 g) curry powder

1 container (6 ounces, or 170 g) plain nondairy yogurt

1 cup (120 g) whole wheat flour

Salt and pepper

Olive oil, for frying (optional)

DIRECTIONS:

In a stockpot, bring the salted water and split peas to a boil, lower the heat to a simmer, and cook until the peas are tender, about 30 minutes, or until most of the moisture is absorbed. You can prepare the peas ahead of time if you prefer.

In a large bowl, combine the peas, sesame oil, curry powder, yogurt, flour, and salt and pepper to taste, and mash with your hands. Form into 4 to 6 patties.

Although you can bake these (350°F [180°C, or gas mark 4] for 15 minutes per side, covered in a foil tent), do yourself a favor and panfry them in olive oil for 3 to 5 minutes per side, or until a nice crispy, golden brown crust forms.

YIELD: 4 TO 6 BURGERS

SERVING SUGGESTION

Serve piping hot on a piece of flatbread or pita with some Tzatziki Sauce (page 193).

23 Curried Chickpea and Broccoli Burger

SOY FREE

A chapter full of burgers inspired by the Middle East just wouldn't be complete without a recipe full of chickpeas and curry!

INGREDIENTS:

2 cans (30 ounces, or 840 g) chickpeas, drained and rinsed

1 tablespoon (15 g) minced garlic

2 tablespoons (32 g) tahini paste

1 tablespoon (15 ml) sesame oil

1 teaspoon green curry paste (you can use yellow curry powder for this as well, but it will be a bit milder)

½ cup (72 g) vital wheat gluten flour

Salt and pepper

1 cup (71 g) broccoli florets, steamed and chopped

Oil, for frying (optional)

SERVING SUGGESTION

This one tastes great even without a bun. A great way to serve it is in a pita or flatbread with Tangy Tahini Sauce (page 182). Serve alongside other Middle Eastern sides, such as dahl, saffron rice, or steamed veggies.

DIRECTIONS:

In a mixing bowl, combine the chickpeas, garlic, tahini, oil, curry paste, flour, and salt and pepper to taste.

Using your hands, mash everything together as if your life depended on it. (Alternatively, you can use a food processor to mix the ingredients together. Just pulse a few times so that everything is combined but still a little chunky.)

After you've mashed everything, add the broccoli and gently combine so it is evenly distributed. If your dough seems too wet, add a little more flour. If your dough seems too dry, add a little more sesame oil. Refrigerate for at least 20 minutes to thicken up a bit.

Form into 6 to 8 patties and cook as desired. These taste good baked or fried. If frying, sauté for 4 to 5 minutes per side, until golden and crispy. If baking, use a baking sheet or baking pan covering with a foil tent to keep in the moisture, and bake for 15 minutes at 350°F (180°C, or gas mark 4), then flip and bake 15 minutes longer, or until firm and just beginning to brown. Or you can bake them for 15 minutes, and then fry them . . . *mmmm.*

YIELD: 6 TO 8 BURGERS

Lizzy's Lentil Daal Burger

My world-traveling friends Lizzy and Tony have introduced me to many wonderful ethnic foods over the years. Going out to dinner or visiting their place for a home-cooked meal is always an exotic treat for the tastebuds. In fact, it was their love of exciting and out-of-the-ordinary cuisine that inspired me to make this lovely little lentil burger with international flair.

INGREDIENTS:

¼ cup (48 g) dried red lentils*

¼ cup (48 g) dried green lentils

¼ cup (56 g) dried split peas

1 pound (454 g) red potatoes, skin on, cut into chunks

2 tablespoons (30 ml) sesame oil

1 yellow onion, diced

4 cloves garlic, minced

1 teaspoon cumin

1 teaspoon coriander

1 teaspoon garam masala

¼ teaspoon turmeric

¼ to ½ cup (30 to 60 g) chickpea flour

Oil, for frying (optional)

*If you can't get red lentils, it's okay—just use all green.

SERVING SUGGESTION

These taste good on their own and would make a nice accompaniment to any Indian-style meal with basmati rice. You can also serve them on a bun with Tangy Tahini Sauce (page 182) or Tzatziki Sauce (page 193).

DIRECTIONS:

Fill a large pot with salted water and add the lentils and split peas. Bring to a boil. Boil for 15 minutes, then add the potatoes. Boil for 15 minutes longer, or until the potatoes are fork-tender.

Meanwhile, heat the oil in a skillet and sauté the onion and garlic until translucent, 5 to 7 minutes. Add the cumin, coriander, garam masala, and turmeric, stir to combine, and sauté for 2 or 3 more minutes.

After the lentils and potatoes are done, strain and return them to the pot. Add the onion and garlic mixture. With a hand potato masher, mash all the ingredients together.

Let sit or refrigerate until cool, at least 20 minutes, or even overnight.

Preheat the oven to 350°F (180°C, or gas mark 4). Line a baking sheet with parchment or a silicone mat, or spray with cooking spray.

Add the flour to the mixture, starting with ¼ cup (30 g) and adding more if needed. Knead until the flour is well incorporated. Form into 8 patties and place on the prepared baking sheet.

Bake for 15 minutes per side, covered in a foil tent, until firm and warmed all the way through. These can also be fried, but I prefer them baked.

YIELD: 8 BURGERS

Masa Masala Burger

WHEAT FREE **SOY FREE**

Two of my favorite ethnic foods are Mexican and Middle Eastern, so why not join the two in a burger? Genius, I say!

INGREDIENTS:

1 cup (114 g) masa harina flour (I like Maseca brand)

1 cup (198 g) fully cooked lentils

⅔ cup (160 ml) water

2 tablespoons (30 ml) olive oil, plus more for frying (optional)

1 teaspoon garam masala

½ teaspoon cumin

⅛ teaspoon sea salt

Freshly cracked black pepper

DIRECTIONS:

This couldn't be easier. Mix all the ingredients together and form into 4 patties.

Panfry in oil (or you can use a little nonstick spray on a hot skillet) and fry for 3 to 5 minutes per side. You can also bake these, but they tend to dry out a bit, so be sure to use a foil tent and maybe even brush a little extra olive oil on them before baking. Bake at 350°F (180°C, or gas mark 4) for about 10 minutes per side.

YIELD: 4 BURGERS

SERVING SUGGESTION

Serve on a Sweet Potato Bun (page 201, and pictured here) alongside a nice big pile of brown rice, lentils, and peas mixed with some Tangy Tahini Sauce (page 182), as shown here.

26 Tabbouleh Burger

SOY FREE

Tabbouleh, tabouli, tabouleh, taboolee . . . however you wanna spell it, it spells YUM! It has a clean, light flavor that just tastes healthy. If you have a food processor, now is the time to use it.

FOR TABBOULEH SALAD:

3 cups (705 ml) water

1 cup (176 g) uncooked bulgur wheat

3 cups (180 g) finely chopped fresh parsley

1 large cucumber, seeded and diced (about 2 cups [270 g])

1 cup (180 g) diced tomatoes (approx. 2 seeded tomatoes)

¼ cup (12 g) finely chopped mint leaves

½ cup (120 ml) olive oil

3 tablespoons (45 g) minced garlic

3 tablespoons (45 ml) lemon juice

Salt and pepper

FOR BURGERS:

1 recipe Tabbouleh Salad (above)

1 cup (120 g) whole wheat flour

3 tablespoons (24 g) cornstarch

2 tablespoons (30 ml) sesame oil (optional)

SERVING SUGGESTION

You can eat this patty warm or cold. I like it all by itself, but it's also super yummy in a pita or on flatbread. It's also good on a wheat bun with a schmear of hummus or Tzatziki Sauce (page 193).

DIRECTIONS:

To make the tabbouleh salad: Bring a pot of lightly salted water to a boil. Add the bulgur wheat, lower the heat to a simmer, and cook, uncovered, for about 10 minutes, or until all the liquid is absorbed. Set aside to cool.

In a large bowl, combine the parsley, cucumber, tomatoes, mint, olive oil, garlic, lemon juice, salt, and pepper to taste. Add the cooled bulgur and mix thoroughly.

Stop here and you have a very perfect tabbouleh salad. You don't have to make it into burgers. I'm okay with that. It won't hurt my feelings. Or you can reserve half as a salad and make the rest into burgers, which is what I usually do because this recipe yields 10 patties! (If you do this, just cut the remaining ingredients in half.)

To make the burgers: Preheat the oven to 350°F (180°C, or gas mark 4). Line a baking pan with parchment or a silicone baking mat.

Add the flour and cornstarch to the Tabbouleh Salad mixture. Knead until well incorporated. If your mixture is too wet, add a little more flour.

Form into 10 patties. Bake for 40 to 45 minutes, flipping halfway through, until firm and just beginning to brown. You can eat them just like this, but they get extra yummy if you panfry them in a little sesame oil after you bake them, just to get a little golden crispy crust!

YIELD: 10 BURGERS

27 Curried Macadamia Nut–Crusted Tofu Burger

If Wendy's serves square burgers, why can't I? I first made these burgers after returning home from a week in beautiful Ka'anapali on the island of Maui. I couldn't get enough macadamia nuts and was making dishes with them daily. I love this burger because it tastes great as a sandwich, but also works great as a main dish, sans the bun.

INGREDIENTS:

12 ounces (340 g) extra-firm tofu, drained and pressed

1 cup (115 g) panko bread crumbs

2 tablespoons (12 g) yellow curry powder

⅓ cup (44 g) chopped dry-roasted macadamia nuts

1 teaspoon paprika

¼ teaspoon sea salt

¼ teaspoon freshly cracked black pepper

1 can (14 ounces, or 414 ml) full-fat coconut milk

SERVING SUGGESTION

Serve on a toasted bun with a schmear of Indian-Spiced Mayo (page 183).

DIRECTIONS:

Preheat the oven to 350°F (180°C, or gas mark 4). Line a baking sheet with parchment or a silicone mat, or spray with cooking spray.

Carefully cut the tofu into 4 equal "steaks."

In a shallow dish, combine the bread crumbs, curry powder, nuts, paprika, salt, and pepper. Pour the coconut milk into a separate shallow dish.

Dip the tofu into the coconut milk, and then dredge in the bread crumb mixture to coat. Repeat with the other 3 pieces and place on the prepared baking sheet.

Bake for about 30 minutes, or until firm and just beginning to brown.

YIELD: 4 BURGERS

Potato Samosa Burger

I could totally sit on the couch, cuddled up under a warm blanket in my fuzzy slippers, watching the Lifetime channel, while popping samosa after samosa in my mouth. This burger is just like the real thing . . . sans the crust!

INGREDIENTS:

1½ pounds (682 g) russet potatoes, washed (peeled if desired)

1 cup (160 g) diced onion

1 teaspoon ground ginger

1 teaspoon ground coriander

1 teaspoon garam masala

1 teaspoon ground cumin

1 hot green chile pepper, such as a jalapeño, seeded and diced

3 tablespoons (45 ml) sesame oil

1½ cups (200 g) fresh or frozen green peas

Salt and pepper

Olive oil, for frying

DIRECTIONS:

Bring a large pot of water to a boil. Cut the potatoes into chunks about 1 inch (2.5 cm). I like to leave the skins on, but that's your call. Boil the potatoes until fork-tender. Drain and return to the pot.

Add the onion, ginger, coriander, garam masala, cumin, chile pepper, and sesame oil and mash with a hand masher or your hands. Carefully mix in the peas, trying not to smash them too much.

Form into 6 to 8 patties.

Panfry in plenty of oil for 3 to 5 minutes per side, or until a nice golden crispy crust forms.

YIELD: 6 TO 8 BURGERS

SERVING SUGGESTION

Enjoy as you would any samosa. I like to have mine with a side of traditional chana masala and saffron rice. These also work well in a pita with hummus and spinach.

Falafel Burger

SOY FREE

These may not be the ball shape you are used to, but they certainly do pop with all of the falafel flavors you know and love.

INGREDIENTS:

2 cups (480 g) fully cooked chickpeas (I use canned)

1 cup (235 ml) vegetable broth

1 cup (160 g) diced onion

2 tablespoons (24 g) potato starch dissolved in ¼ cup (60 ml) water to make a slurry

⅓ cup (80 ml) olive oil, plus more for frying

½ cup (8 g) finely chopped fresh cilantro (or parsley [30 g] for you cilantro haters!)

1 teaspoon ground coriander

½ teaspoon ground cumin

½ teaspoon cayenne pepper

2 tablespoons (30 ml) lemon juice

1 cup (120 g) whole wheat flour

1½ to 2 cups (180 to 240 g) chickpea flour

Salt and pepper

SERVING SUGGESTION

Serve in a pita with Tzatziki Sauce (page 193) and some fresh, crunchy vegetables, as shown here.

DIRECTIONS:

Combine the chickpeas, vegetable broth, and onion in a large pot. Bring to a boil, lower the heat to a simmer, and simmer, uncovered, for 15 minutes.

Mix in the potato starch slurry, remove from the heat, and stir well to thicken. Transfer to a mixing bowl and mash with a fork or potato masher.

Add the ⅓ cup (80 ml) olive oil, cilantro, coriander, cumin, cayenne, lemon juice, whole wheat flour, 1½ cups (180 g) of the chickpea flour, and salt and pepper to taste. Knead until a nice elastic dough is formed, adding some of the remaining ½ cup (60 g) chickpea flour, a little bit at a time, if your dough is too sticky.

Preheat the oven to 350°F (180°C, or gas mark 4) and line a baking sheet with parchment or a silicone mat.

Form into 6 patties and place on the prepared baking sheet.

Bake for 20 minutes, uncovered.

Preheat a pan with olive oil and panfry the baked burgers for 3 to 5 minutes per side to get a nice golden crispy crust. A panini press or tabletop electric grill (like a George Foreman) also works well as an alternative to frying after you bake it.

YIELD: 6 BURGERS

CHAPTER 5

BURGERS FROM THE BOOT

TASTY BURGERS INFLUENCED BY THE FLAVORS OF ITALY

30 Sun-Dried Tomato and Pesto Burger

WHEAT FREE **SOY FREE**

I made this recipe wheat-free by using brown rice flour, but if you do not have a wheat allergy, feel free to use whole wheat flour instead.

INGREDIENTS:

1 tablespoon (15 ml) olive oil, plus more for frying (optional)

8 ounces (227 g) mushrooms, sliced or chopped

1 white or yellow onion, chopped

¼ cup (28 g) sun-dried tomato pieces, packed in oil, drained

2 cups (330 g) cooked brown rice

1 recipe Simple Pesto (page 186)

Salt and pepper

½ to 1 cup (80 to 160 g) brown rice flour

SERVING SUGGESTION

This one is good on two crusty pieces of Italian bread, grilled like a panini, but that kind of takes away from the soy- and wheat-freeness unless you have access to wheat-free bread. I like it on said bread, schmeared with extra pesto and a few fresh leaves of spinach. If it's for lunch, serve it with an Italian pasta salad; for dinner, serve it along with a nice bowl of tomato soup.

DIRECTIONS:

In a skillet, heat the 1 tablespoon (15 ml) olive oil and sauté the mushrooms and onion over medium-high heat for 7 to 10 minutes, or until fragrant, translucent, and reduced by half.

Add the sautéed onion and mushrooms, tomato pieces, rice, pesto, and salt and pepper to taste to a food processor and pulse until well combined but still a little chunky. Transfer to a mixing bowl.

Depending on the moisture content of your mixture, knead in the flour a little at a time until a good consistency for forming patties is reached. Refrigerate for at least 20 minutes, so the flour can absorb the flavors and moisture of the mixture.

Form into 8 patties and cook as desired.

If baking, use a baking sheet lined with parchment or a silicone baking mat, and bake at 350°F (180°C, or gas mark 4) for 15 minutes, then flip and bake for 15 minutes longer, until firm and just beginning to brown. If frying, make sure there is enough oil in the pan to prevent it from sticking and fry over medium-high heat for 4 to 5 minutes per side, or until a nice golden crust forms.

YIELD: 8 BURGERS

Fire-Roasted Red Pepper Burger

WHEAT FREE   **SOY FREE**

Über-Super-Mega-Awesome Tester Liz had a burger at a restaurant that she *loved* and asked me to try and recreate it. This one's for Liz.

INGREDIENTS:

1 can (15 ounces, or 420 g) chickpeas, with liquid

3 or 4 cloves garlic

1 red bell pepper

2 tablespoons (32 g) tahini paste

2 tablespoons (30 ml) sesame oil

2 tablespoons (30 ml) lemon juice

Salt and pepper

2 cups (240 g) chickpea flour

Oil, for frying (optional)

SERVING SUGGESTION

I actually think this patty stands well on its own as a main dish, but it's also good on a crusty whole wheat bun or tucked inside pita and garnished with fresh greens and a goddess-type tahini dressing.

DIRECTIONS:

Empty the can of chickpeas, along with the liquid, into a saucepan, add the garlic, bring to a boil, lower the heat to a simmer, and simmer for 15 to 20 minutes.

While the beans are simmering, roast the bell pepper. Using tongs, place the entire pepper on an open flame. Your gas stove burner works perfect for this. Roast it until it is blackened and soft. Let cool and remove the seeds and stem.

After the beans are done simmering, strain out the liquid, reserving the garlic.

To a food processor or blender, add the beans, garlic, seeded fire-roasted pepper, tahini, sesame oil, lemon juice, and salt and pepper to taste. Blend until smooth.

Transfer to a bowl and add the flour, ½ cup (60 g) at a time, until a patty-able consistency is reached. Depending on the moisture content of your beans and pepper, more or less flour may be needed.

Form into 4 patties and cook as desired. Fry in oil for 3 to 5 minutes per side, or until golden brown and crispy, or bake on a baking sheet lined with parchment or a silicone baking mat at 350°F (180°C, or gas mark 4) for 15 to 20 minutes per side, covered in a foil tent to retain moisture, until firm and warmed all the way through.

YIELD: 4 BURGERS

32 Zucchini Mushroom Burger

These burgers are nice and juicy and full of flavor, just as a burger should be. I like these better fried than baked.

INGREDIENTS:

2 tablespoons (30 ml) olive oil, plus more for frying (optional)

8 ounces (227 g) mushrooms (I used white buttons, but portobellos would be yummy here, too), chopped or sliced

1 yellow or white onion, chopped

2 tablespoons (30 g) minced garlic

1 cup (235 ml) vegetable broth

1 cup (96 g) TVP granules

1 cup (124 g) grated or shredded zucchini

2½ tablespoons (19 g) ground flaxseed mixed with 3 tablespoons (45 ml) warm water

1 cup (144 g) vital wheat gluten flour

Salt and pepper

SERVING SUGGESTION

I serve this on a hearty wheat bun topped with Chunky Marinara (page 188). I'm not a big fan of many vegan cheeses, but a nice pile of Daiya Mozzarella might just be tasty on this guy. Serve with a side of Fried Zucchini (page 207) and additional marinara to dip 'em in.

DIRECTIONS:

Heat the 2 tablespoons (30 ml) olive oil in a pan and sauté the mushrooms, onion, and garlic until reduced by half, slightly browned, and fragrant, 7 to 10 minutes.

Add the vegetable broth and bring to a simmer.

Add the TVP granules, stir to combine, cover, and remove from the heat. Let sit for 10 minutes.

When cool enough to handle, transfer to a mixing bowl and add the zucchini, flax mixture, flour, and salt and pepper to taste. Knead with your hands until very well incorporated. Depending on the amount of moisture in your vegetables, you may need to add a little extra flour. Cover and refrigerate for at least 20 minutes to thicken up a bit.

Form into 8 patties and cook as desired.

If frying, use a heavy-bottom skillet with plenty of oil and fry for 3 to 4 minutes per side, or until golden and crispy. If baking, use a baking sheet lined with parchment or a silicone baking mat, and bake, covered in a foil tent, at 350°F (180°C, or gas mark 4) for 15 to 20 minutes per side, until firm and just beginning to brown.

YIELD: 8 BURGERS

RECIPE NOTE

When I make these I like to leave the mushrooms really big and chunky so that I can bite into them. Feel free to leave them big or chop them into tiny bits depending on your tastes.

Couscous Pantry Burger

33

The reason these are called pantry burgers is because I developed this recipe as I was conducting "The Great Grocery Experiment." Inspired by my cousin, Leah, and her husband, Tim, I set out to go a month without buying any food, using only what I already had in my kitchen. Each time I created a new and noteworthy dish, I dubbed it a "pantry" dish. And if only for this burger alone, it was a worthwhile experiment!

INGREDIENTS:

2 cups (470 ml) vegetable broth

1 can (14 ounces, or 392 g) tomato sauce

1 cup (174 g) dry couscous

1 cup (96 g) TVP granules

1 tablespoon (2 g) dried basil or 3 tablespoons (9 g) fresh, finely chopped

2 tablespoons (30 g) minced garlic

¼ cup (31 g) shredded or grated zucchini

2½ tablespoons (19 g) ground flaxseed mixed with 3 tablespoons (45 ml) warm water

1 cup (120 g) whole wheat pastry flour

¼ cup (30 g) nutritional yeast

2 tablespoons (30 ml) olive oil, plus extra for frying

DIRECTIONS:

Bring the vegetable broth and tomato sauce to a boil. Lower the heat to a simmer. Add the couscous and TVP, stir well, cover, and remove from the heat. Let sit for 10 minutes to absorb all of the liquid.

When cool enough to handle, add the basil, garlic, zucchini, flaxseed mixture, flour, nutritional yeast, and 2 tablespoons (30 ml) oil. Mix together and knead well so that all ingredients are well incorporated and a nice patty-able consistency is reached.

Form into 8 patties and fry in oil for 3 to 5 minutes per side, until golden and crispy. I don't recommend baking these, because they get pretty dry.

YIELD: 8 BURGERS

SERVING SUGGESTION

If you like vegan cheeses, a slice of nondairy mozzarella would work well here. Also, top with some roasted garlic or Aioli Dipping Sauce (page 189). A bit of Chunky Marinara (page 188) would be tasty, too. Fried Zucchini (page 207) would be a perfect side dish with these. The perfect bun? Try the Rustica Bun on page 199.

34 Pizza Burger

Pepperoni pizza as a burger? Whhaaaat? Remember to adjust the spiciness according to your taste buds. I'm of the school that they call it "pepper"oni for a reason, so as written, it can be pretty spicy! If you want to save any ground pepperoni for your next pizza pie, simply set some aside after reconstituting the TVP (or make double!).

INGREDIENTS:

1 tablespoon (8 g) freshly ground black pepper

1 tablespoon (7 g) paprika

1 teaspoon whole aniseed

1 teaspoon salt

1 teaspoon red pepper flakes

1 teaspoon sugar

1 teaspoon dried basil

1 teaspoon chipotle powder or cayenne pepper

1 tablespoon (8 g) garlic powder

1 cup (96 g) TVP granules

1 cup (235 ml) water

2 tablespoons (30 ml) liquid smoke

2 tablespoons (30 ml) plus ¼ cup (60 ml) olive oil, divided

6 ounces (170 g) tomato paste

1 cup (144 g) vital wheat gluten flour

⅓ cup (80 g) nondairy sour cream, store-bought or homemade (page 191)

Oil, for frying (optional)

DIRECTIONS:

In a microwave-safe dish, combine the pepper, paprika, aniseed, salt, red pepper flakes, sugar, basil, chipotle powder, garlic powder, TVP, water, liquid smoke, and 2 tablespoons (30 ml) olive oil. Cover tightly with plastic wrap and microwave on high for 5 to 6 minutes. Alternatively, bring the water to a boil and pour over the TVP mixed with the spices, oil, and liquid smoke, cover, and let sit for 10 minutes. Let cool.

Add the tomato paste, flour, remaining ¼ cup (60 g) oil, and sour cream to the cooled TVP mixture. Using your hands, mash everything together and form into 6 patties.

You can fry or bake these with great results. Panfry in just a smidge of oil for 5 minutes per side over medium-high heat, or until a nice crispy crust forms. Or bake them at 350°F (180°C, or gas mark 4) on a baking sheet lined with parchment or a silicone baking mat, uncovered, for 30 minutes, flipping halfway through.

YIELD: 6 BURGERS

SERVING SUGGESTION

For extra pizza goodness, place some shredded vegan mozzarella on the top of your burger during the last few minutes of cooking to get it all nice and melty. For a bun? Try garlic naan or 50/50 Flatbread (page 197, and pictured here), schmeared with Simple Pesto (page 186, and pictured here).

35 Mushroom, Asparagus, and Spinach Burger

SOY FREE

Here's a nice simple veggie burger, with . . . wait for it . . . lots of veggies!

INGREDIENTS:

3 cups (705 ml) vegetable broth

8 ounces (227 g) mushrooms, sliced or chopped

1 onion, diced

1 cup (108 g) shredded carrots

2 teaspoons (10 g) minced garlic

1 cup (190 g) uncooked brown rice

1 cup (134 g) chopped asparagus spears (½-inch [1.3 cm] pieces)

2 cups (60 g) chiffonaded spinach leaves

2 tablespoons (8 g) chopped fresh dill

1 cup (80 g) uncooked quick-cooking oats

½ cup (65 g) ground raw cashews

1 cup (120 g) whole wheat flour

½ cup (72 g) vital wheat gluten flour

Salt and pepper

Oil, for frying (optional)

DIRECTIONS:

To a large pot, add the vegetable broth, mushrooms, onion, carrots, and garlic. Bring to a boil. Lower the heat to a simmer and stir in the rice. Cover and simmer for about 20 minutes, or until the rice is fully cooked.

Uncover and stir in the asparagus, spinach, and dill. Continue to cook, uncovered, until most of the moisture has been absorbed.

Remove from the heat, stir in the oats, cover, and let sit for 10 minutes.

Mix in the cashews, whole wheat flour, gluten flour, and salt and pepper to taste. Mix until all ingredients are well incorporated. Use your hands if necessary. Cover and refrigerate for at least 20 minutes to thicken up a bit.

Meanwhile, preheat the oven to 350°F (180°C, or gas mark 4). Line a baking sheet with parchment paper or a silicone baking mat.

Form into 8 to 10 patties, place on the prepared baking sheet, and bake for 20 minutes, until firm and warmed all the way through. If desired, you can fry these after baking, to give them a nice crispy crust.

YIELD: 8 TO 10 BURGERS

SERVING SUGGESTION

Chock-full of veggies, this one doesn't need much. Place on a nice wheat bun with some crispy greens and a schmear of vegan mayo (page 191) and you're good to go.

Sun-Dried Tomato and Artichoke Burger

Feel free to cut this recipe in half. I just hate to use half of a can of anything, because I know I will forget to use the other half and it'll go bad. The patties freeze well, however, and reheat nicely for lunches.

INGREDIENTS:

2 tablespoons (30 ml) olive oil*

8 ounces (227 g) mushrooms, sliced

1 yellow onion, roughly chopped

2 tablespoons (30 g) minced garlic

Pinch of salt

1 can (14 ounces, or 392 g) artichoke hearts, drained

¼ cup (28 g) sun-dried tomatoes, packed in oil

6 ounces (170 g) roasted red peppers, store-bought or homemade (see page 69)

¼ cup (30 g) nutritional yeast

2 cups (160 g) quick-cooking oats

3 cups (495 g) cooked brown rice**

Oil, for frying (optional)

If trying to cut down on added fats, use nonstick cooking spray or a Misto filled with olive oil.

**I find that using vegetable broth instead of water when preparing the rice gives it a wonderful flavor.*

DIRECTIONS:

In a cast-iron skillet, heat the oil over medium-high heat and add the mushrooms, onion, garlic, and salt. Sauté for 5 to 7 minutes, or until very fragrant, translucent, and reduced by about half.

In a food processor, combine the artichokes, sun-dried tomatoes, peppers, nutritional yeast, oats, and rice. Add the sautéed mixture. Process until a uniform consistency is achieved. Transfer to a bowl and refrigerate for about 1 hour. This will allow the oats to absorb a lot of the moisture and make the patties easier to form.

Depending on the moisture content of your mix, you may want to add a little more or less oats.

Form into 8 to 10 patties and cook as desired. These are a bit on the mushy side when pan-fried. Baking seems to stiffen them up a little bit more. But, even mushy, they taste really delicious.

Panfry in oil over medium heat for 5 to 7 minutes per side, or until nice and crispy, or bake, loosely covered in a foil tent, at 350°F (180°C, or gas mark 4) for 15 minutes per side, or until firm and just beginning to brown.

YIELD: 8 TO 10 BURGERS

SERVING SUGGESTION

Serve on toasted crusty bread or a roll with a schmear of Garlic Artichoke Spread (page 188) or hummus and mixed greens. On the side? A nice green vegetable, such as broccoli, green beans, or asparagus.

Broosketta Burger

I so enjoy the bruschetta topping on this burger that I often make it to mix with pasta or simply serve over crostini.

FOR BRUSCHETTA TOPPING:

12 ounces (340 g) extra-firm tofu, drained and pressed

20 leaves fresh basil, cut into chiffonade

2 tablespoons (30 g) minced garlic

¼ cup (60 ml) olive oil

1 cup (180 g) diced Roma tomatoes, seeded

Salt and pepper, to taste

FOR BURGERS:

1 cup (96 g) TVP granules

1 cup (235 ml) vegetable broth

½ cup (72 g) vital wheat gluten flour

½ cup plus 2 tablespoons (6 ounces, or 170 g) tomato paste

¼ cup (30 g) nutritional yeast

1 cup (259 g) Bruschetta Topping (above), plus extra for serving

Salt and pepper

DIRECTIONS:

To make the topping: Chop the tofu into tiny, tiny cubes, about ⅛ inch (3 mm), if possible. Mix together all the ingredients and let sit for a few hours to really let the flavors meld.

To make the burgers: Preheat the oven to 350°F (180°C, or gas mark 4). Line a baking sheet with parchment or a silicone baking mat.

In a microwave-safe bowl, mix together the TVP granules and the broth, cover tightly with plastic wrap, and microwave for 5 to 6 minutes. Alternatively, bring the broth to a boil, pour over the TVP, cover, and let sit for 10 minutes.

Combine the reconstituted TVP, flour, tomato paste, nutritional yeast, Bruschetta Topping, and salt and pepper. Use your hands to really mush it all together. Form into 6 patties and place on the prepared baking sheet.

Bake, uncovered, for 15 minutes, then flip and bake for 15 minutes longer.

Top with a pile of extra bruschetta.

YIELD: 6 BURGERS

SERVING SUGGESTION

Serve on a toasted piece of Italian bread, or better yet, garlic bread, piled high with a generous helping of bruschetta topping, as shown here.

38 Fresh from the Mediterranean Burger

Full of fresh Mediterranean flavor, these burgers are sure to please even the most critical of eaters.

FOR BURGERS:

1 cup (96 g) TVP granules

1 cup (235 ml) vegetable broth

6 ounces (170 g) extra-firm tofu, drained, pressed, and crumbled

2 teaspoons (6 g) capers, drained

2 teaspoons (2.5 g) minced fresh oregano

2 teaspoons (1.5 g) fresh rosemary, finely chopped

¾ teaspoon freshly ground black pepper

1 tablespoon (6 g) lemon zest

1 cup (144 g) vital wheat gluten flour

FOR OLIVE SPREAD:

12 kalamata olives, pitted

1 tablespoon (4 g) chopped fresh dill

1 tablespoon (4 g) chopped fresh parsley

2 tablespoons (30 ml) fresh lemon juice

¼ teaspoon agave nectar

¼ cup (60 ml) olive oil

1 large tomato, seeded

¼ cucumber, peeled and seeded

½ red onion

DIRECTIONS:

To make the burgers: Preheat the oven to 350°F (180°C, or gas mark 4). Line a baking sheet with parchment or a silicone baking mat.

In a microwave-safe bowl, mix together the TVP granules and broth, cover tightly with plastic wrap, and microwave for 5 to 6 minutes. Alternatively, bring the broth to a boil, pour over the TVP, cover, and let stand for 10 minutes. Carefully remove from the microwave, remove the plastic wrap, and let cool.

Transfer to a mixing bowl and add the tofu, capers, oregano, rosemary, pepper, zest, and flour. Using your hands, knead until a nice patty-able consistency is reached. Form into 4 patties and place on the prepared baking sheet.

Bake, uncovered for 30 minutes, flipping halfway through.

To make the olive spread: Add all the ingredients to a food processor and pulse a few times until combined, but still chunky.

Smear a nice thick coating of spread on both sides of a bun before sandwiching the burgers.

YIELD: 4 LARGE BURGERS

SERVING SUGGESTION

Serve on a crusty roll, lightly toasted, with Tabbouleh Salad (page 60).

Ravioli Burger

These ravioli burgers make gigantic raviolis that will have your guests wide-eyed with amazement.

FOR RAViOLi PASTA DOUGH:

1½ cups (180 g) semolina flour

2 tablespoons (30 ml) olive oil

½ cup (120 ml) water

Pinch of salt

FOR BURGERS:

1 cup (96 g) TVP granules

1 cup (235 ml) vegetable broth

14 ounces (392 g) extra-firm tofu, drained, pressed, and crumbled

¼ cup (30 g) nutritional yeast

2 tablespoons (33 g) tomato paste

2 tablespoons (30 ml) olive oil

1 tablespoon (6 g) whole fennel seeds

1 teaspoon garlic powder

Salt and pepper

DiRECTiONS:

To make the ravioli pasta dough: Combine all the ingredients and knead for about 5 minutes until nice and smooth. Divide into 2 pieces and roll out to about ⅛ inch (3 mm) thick. Using a lid, a small saucer, or a cookie cutter, cut out 8 rounds about 5 inches (12.5 cm) in diameter. Set the rounds in a single layer to dry out a bit while you assemble the burgers.

To make the burgers: Mix all the ingredients together until well incorporated. Form into 4 patties.

Assemble the raviolis by sandwiching one patty between two rounds of dough and pinching the edges together to seal. Repeat with the other three patties.

Bring a large pot of water to a boil. Boil each ravioli burger for 4 minutes, or until the pasta is tender. Drain.

At this point, you can top with your favorite sauce, or you can place your Ravioli Burgers in a baking dish, in a single layer, top with sauce, and bake for 10 to 15 minutes at 350°F (180°C, or gas mark 4).

YiELD: 4 BURGERS

SERViNG SUGGESTiON

Serve topped with your favorite pasta sauce and a side of toasted garlic bread.

CHAPTER 6

BURGERS FROM THE HEARTLAND

BURGERS INSPIRED BY THE TRADITIONS OF THE GOOD OLE U.S. OF A.

40 All-American Burger

Here's a plain old burger that stands up to the grill with the best of its meaty cousins.

INGREDIENTS:

2 tablespoons (30 ml) olive oil, plus more for frying (optional)

8 ounces (227 g) mushrooms, sliced or chopped

3 cloves garlic, minced

¾ cup (180 ml) vegetable broth

1 cup (96 g) TVP granules

¼ cup (30 g) nutritional yeast

½ cup (72 g) vital wheat gluten flour

1 tablespoon (8 g) ground mustard

1 tablespoon (8 g) onion powder

¼ teaspoon liquid smoke (optional)

Salt and pepper

SERVING SUGGESTION

Garnish as you would any burger. I just eat mine plain with a smidge of vegan mayo (page 191) on the bun. Add a slice of vegan cheese for an All-American Cheeseburger.

DIRECTIONS:

In a heavy-bottom skillet, heat the oil and sauté the mushrooms and garlic for 5 to 7 minutes, or until fragrant and translucent.

Add the vegetable broth and bring to a simmer.

Add the TVP granules, mix well, cover, and remove from the heat. Let sit for 10 minutes.

When cool enough to handle, add the nutritional yeast, flour, ground mustard, onion powder, liquid smoke, and salt and pepper to taste and mix well using your hands.

Place in the fridge to cool for about 20 minutes. This will help the dough stiffen up a bit.

Form into 4 patties and cook as desired.

I grill these on the barbecue with no foil and it stands up just fine. I cook them on a pretty hot spot on the grill for about 4 to 5 minutes on each side. I did rub a little extra oil on the patty before grilling to help prevent sticking.

They can also be fried in a skillet with a little oil for the same amount of time. I like the way the grilled ones come out better than the fried.

YIELD: 4 BURGERS

The State Fair Cheeseburger

Deep-fried and delicious! That's what fair food's all about, right? Inspired by deep-fried Twinkies and beer-battered potatoes, this cheeseburger is all about the batter, baby! (See www.barnivore.com to check the veganness of your booze!)

INGREDIENTS:

Oil, for frying

¾ cup (90 g) all-purpose flour

¾ cup (105 g) yellow cornmeal

1 cup (235 ml) vegan beer

2 tablespoons (30 ml) vegetable oil

1 tablespoon (21 g) agave nectar

1 teaspoon Dijon mustard

½ teaspoon baking soda

½ teaspoon baking powder

¼ teaspoon paprika

1 recipe Inside-Out Cheeseburger Seitanic Stuffer (page 55), adding 1 tablespoon (6 g) imitation bacon bits, store-bought or homemade (page 185), to the centers of each burger

DIRECTIONS:

If you have a deep fryer, now is a good time to use it. If not, using a pot filled with 4 inches (10 cm) of oil will do the trick just fine.

Preheat the oil to 350°F (180°C). Have ready a plate or tray lined with paper towels.

In a shallow dish, mix together the flour, cornmeal, beer, vegetable oil, agave, mustard, baking soda, baking powder, and paprika until smooth.

Dip each Inside-Out Cheeseburger Seitanic Stuffer into the batter to coat.

Using tongs, carefully submerge the battered burger in the hot oil to fry until golden and crispy, about 1 minute.

Transfer to the prepared plate to drain excess oil.

YIELD: 6 BURGERS

SERVING SUGGESTION

Please do yourself a favor and eat some greens along with this! I really don't care what kind: kale, spinach, broccoli, or even a plain ol' garden salad. Anything to counterbalance this cardiac arrest!

42 Scarborough Fair Tofu Burger

WHEAT FREE

If there was ever a reason to call a veggie burger hippie food, then this burger fits the bill. Inspired by watching *The Drug Years* on VH1 and, of course, dear and sweet Simon & Garfunkel, these burgers are sure to please your peace-lovin' pals. Normally, I advocate the use of fresh herbs, but for this one, dried ones work best. I also tend to overspice things, so please, unless you really like the flavors of these herbs, feel free to cut the amounts down.

INGREDIENTS:

1 tablespoon (2 g) dried parsley

1 tablespoon (2 g) dried sage

1 tablespoon (2 g) dried rosemary

1 tablespoon (2 g) dried thyme

12 ounces (340 g) extra-firm tofu, drained and pressed

1 cup (96 g) TVP granules

1 cup (235 ml) vegetable broth

2 tablespoons (30 g) minced garlic

2½ tablespoons (19 g) ground flaxseed mixed with 3 tablespoons (45 ml) water

¼ cup (32 g) hulled sunflower seeds

¼ cup (32 g) hulled pumpkin seeds

Salt and pepper

SERVING SUGGESTION

Serve with herbal tea and a side of granola. Just kidding. This one pairs very nicely with a whole grain bun or bread and a light schmear of Creamy Balsamic Dressing (page 189, and pictured here). Sprouts, avocado, and tomato are also good toppings. It's best served for lunch with a hearty green salad or other veggie.

DIRECTIONS:

Grind the parsley, sage, rosemary, and thyme into a fine powder. I use a coffee grinder for this.

In a mixing bowl, crumble the tofu and mix well with the spice mixture so that the herbs are well infused with the tofu. Let sit for the flavors to meld.

In a microwave-safe bowl, mix together the TVP granules and the broth, cover tightly with plastic wrap, and micro-wave for 5 to 6 minutes. Alternatively, bring the broth to a boil, pour over the TVP, cover, and let sit for 10 minutes.

When cool enough to handle, add the TVP to the tofu mixture, then add the minced garlic, flaxseed mixture, sunflower seeds, pumpkin seeds, and salt and pepper to taste. Mix with your hands until all the ingredients are very well incorporated. The mixture will be nice and smooth, and should form lovely burgers. Shape into 6 patties. Refrigerate until ready to cook, although refrigeration isn't necessary if you plan on cooking them right away.

I recommend baking these rather than frying. It just seems that this burger is too healthy to fry. Preheat the oven to 350°F (180°C, or gas mark 4) and line a baking sheet with parchment or a silicone baking mat. Bake, covered with a foil tent, for 15 minutes per side.

YIELD: 6 BURGERS

43 Really Meaty Burger

If there were an Atkins diet for vegans, this burger would definitely be on the menu! It is the meatiest veggie burger I've ever had. It's a bit labor-intensive, unless you make the seitan ahead of time, but OH MY! They are really meaty.

INGREDIENTS:

1 cup (96 g) TVP granules

¼ cup (60 ml) soy sauce

¾ cup (180 ml) plus ⅓ cup (80 ml) vegetable broth or water, divided

2 tablespoons (30 ml) peanut oil

2 cups (200 g) prepared seitan, store-bought or homemade (page 217), chopped into tiny bits

½ cup (72 g) vital wheat gluten flour

¼ cup (30 g) nutritional yeast

1 tablespoon (8 g) garlic powder

1 tablespoon (8 g) onion powder

Pepper

Oil, for frying (optional)

SERVING SUGGESTION

This one really is a standard meaty burger that goes great with the standard fixin's (ketchup, mustard, lettuce, tomato, vegan mayo [page 191] . . .) and a side of fries.

DIRECTIONS:

In a microwave-safe bowl, mix together the TVP granules, soy sauce, and the ¾ cup (180 ml) broth. Cover tightly with plastic wrap, and microwave for 5 to 6 minutes. Alternatively, bring the soy sauce and broth to a boil, pour over the TVP granules, cover, and let sit for 10 minutes. Place in a large mixing bowl.

Preheat the oil in a frying pan over medium-high heat. Add the seitan and sauté until browned, but not too crispy, about 5 to 7 minutes.

Add the seitan, flour, nutritional yeast, garlic powder, onion powder, and pepper to taste to the TVP mixture. Mix well, using your hands to make sure the flour and spices get fully incorporated. Add the remaining ⅓ cup (80 ml) broth until you get a patty-able consistency.

Form into 6 to 8 patties and cook as desired.

I really like these fried for about 4 to 5 minutes per side until crispy and golden brown.

If baking, cover with a foil tent to keep moist and bake for 15 minutes per side at 350°F (180°C, or gas mark 4), until firm and warmed all the way through.

YIELD: 6 TO 8 BURGERS

Green Castle Sliders

These are really cool, because after you make them, you can just refrigerate the logs and slice them up whenever you want a little burger. You can get at least twenty sliders from this recipe, so it also makes a great appetizer. Alternatively, you can use this spicy seitan in other dishes that call for seitan; just keep in mind that this recipe is a little breadier than Traditional Boiled Seitan (page 217).

INGREDIENTS:

2 cups (288 g) vital wheat gluten flour

2 cups (240 g) whole wheat pastry flour

½ cup (60 g) nutritional yeast

1 tablespoon (6 g) ground black pepper

1 tablespoon (8 g) onion powder

1 tablespoon (8 g) garlic powder

1 tablespoon (7 g) paprika

1 tablespoon (8 g) cayenne pepper

1½ cups (355 ml) water

⅔ cup (160 ml) olive oil

⅔ cup (160 ml) tamari or soy sauce

⅓ cup (94 g) ketchup

DIRECTIONS:

Preheat the oven to 350°F (180°C, or gas mark 4).

In a large bowl, combine the flours, nutritional yeast, black pepper, onion powder, garlic powder, paprika, and cayenne.

In a separate bowl, combine the water, oil, tamari, and ketchup.

Add the wet ingredients to the dry and incorporate well. Using your hands, knead the dough for several minutes. Let sit for about 10 minutes.

Divide the dough into 2 equal pieces.

Maneuver the wet mushy mass into a log shape in the center of a large piece of aluminum foil. Roll it tightly into a log, about 2 inches (5 cm) in diameter, twisting the ends nice and tight. Repeat with the other piece.

Place both logs in the oven, directly on the racks, and bake for 90 minutes.

Remove and let cool, and then unwrap.

Slice into pieces about ½ thick (1.3 cm) and serve.

YIELD: 20 SLIDERS

SERVING SUGGESTION

Serve them up on small dinner rolls as appetizers. For breakfast, serve them on Simple Biscuits (page 198), open-faced and smothered with your favorite gravy. Serve with a side of hash browns or country potatoes.

Bacon Cheeseburger

Okay, this delves into the little bit crazy category. But you know what? These babies taste so good and they are extremely hearty and thick, so they hold together very, very well. One really amazing thing about these is that my very-much-not-a-vegetarian husband took a bite and said, and I quote, "You have a winner here!" Oh my gosh, I almost fell over. I also had a few open-minded omni friends over one night and they agreed. The consensus was that they taste almost exactly like a Carl's Jr. Western Bacon Cheeseburger.

INGREDIENTS:

1 cup (96 g) TVP granules

1 scant cup (225 ml) vegetable broth

¼ cup (25 g) imitation bacon bits, store-bought or homemade (page 185)

1 cup (144 g) vital wheat gluten flour

¼ teaspoon liquid smoke

½ cup (60 g) nutritional yeast

1 tablespoon (8 g) garlic powder

1 tablespoon (8 g) onion powder

¼ cup (64 g) peanut butter

¼ cup (60 ml) pure maple syrup

¼ cup (60 ml) vegetable oil

¼ cup (68 g) barbecue sauce, store-bought or homemade (page 183)

Salt and pepper

Oil, for frying (optional)

DIRECTIONS:

In a large microwave-safe bowl, mix together the TVP granules and the broth, cover tightly with plastic wrap, and microwave for 5 to 6 minutes. Alternatively, bring the broth to a boil, pour over the TVP granules, cover, and let sit for 10 minutes. Let cool.

Add the bacon bits, flour, liquid smoke, nutritional yeast, garlic powder, onion powder, peanut butter, maple syrup, oil, barbecue sauce, and salt and pepper to taste to the bowl. Knead together for at least 5 minutes, then let sit for a few minutes to thicken up.

Form into 4 patties. Refrigerate or freeze until ready to use.

Cook as desired. Panfry in oil for 3 to 5 minutes per side over medium-high heat, or until a nice crispy crust forms. Or bake them at 350°F (180°C, or gas mark 4) on a baking sheet lined with parchment or a silicone baking mat, uncovered, for 30 minutes, flipping halfway through. These are very sturdy and hold up just fine on the grill.

YIELD: 4 BURGERS

SERVING SUGGESTION

I suggest these be served with a dollop of barbecue sauce and a few onion rings, with some baked beans on the side.

46 Basic Black Bean BBQ Burger

This hearty, meaty burger is a great burger to serve up to meat lovers. I know whenever I do, they love 'em and the real burgers get left behind as these get gobbled up.

INGREDIENTS:

1 cup (96 g) TVP granules

1 scant cup (225 ml) water

½ cup (80 g) diced onion

1 can (15 ounces, or 420 g) black beans, drained and rinsed

¾ cup (204 g) barbecue sauce, store-bought or homemade (page 183)

1 tablespoon (8 g) onion powder

1 tablespoon (8 g) garlic powder

1 teaspoon black pepper

3 tablespoons (48 g) peanut butter

½ cup (56 g) soy flour

Oil, for frying (optional)

SERVING SUGGESTION

These taste great at a barbecue on a Plain White Bun (page 196) with a dollop of guacamole. Serve with some Smoky Potato Salad (page 214, and pictured here) and corn on the cob.

DIRECTIONS:

In a microwave-safe bowl, mix together the TVP granules and the water, cover tightly with plastic wrap, and microwave for 5 to 6 minutes. Alternatively, bring the water to a boil, pour over the TVP granules, cover, and let sit for 10 minutes.

When cool enough to handle, mix in the onion, beans, barbecue sauce, onion powder, garlic powder, pepper, peanut butter, and flour. Using your hands, knead the dough to incorporate the ingredients fully, and until the TVP granules are no longer the consistency of granules. This will be about 5 minutes of hand manipulation. If your dough is too dry, add a bit of oil to the mix.

Refrigerate for at least 20 minutes.

Form into 8 patties and cook as desired.

If baking, place on a baking sheet lined with parchment or a silicone baking mat and bake for 30 minutes at 350°F (180°C, or gas mark 4) loosely covered with a foil tent, flipping halfway through.

If frying in oil, cook for 3 to 4 minutes per side, until a nice crispy golden crust forms.

These stand up well on the grill, too!

YIELD: 8 BURGERS

47 Popeye Burger

WHEAT FREE **SOY FREE**

Eat your spinach and you will be strong! I really think the Popeye cartoons were on to something, you know?

INGREDIENTS:

2 cups (380 g) uncooked brown rice

1 can (14 ounces, or 392 g) spinach

1 cup (80 g) quick-cooking oats

½ cup (68 g) raw or toasted pine nuts

1 tablespoon (8 g) garlic powder

1 tablespoon (8 g) onion powder

1 tablespoon (8 g) ground mustard

1 teaspoon dried basil

1 teaspoon sweet paprika

3 tablespoons (45 ml) sesame oil

Salt and pepper

Oil, for frying (optional)

SERVING SUGGESTION

Sun-dried Tomato Aioli (page 187) would be a tasty spread. Strangely enough, I also like these alongside mashed potatoes.

DIRECTIONS:

Prepare the rice in a rice cooker or on the stove according to package directions.

Drain the excess liquid from the spinach and place in a mixing bowl with the oats; let sit while the rice is cooking. The oats will absorb the moisture from the spinach and soften.

When the rice is fully cooked, mix it into the spinach mixture and add the pine nuts, garlic powder, onion powder, mustard, basil, paprika, oil, and salt and pepper to taste.

When it is cool enough to handle, form into 8 patties.

Panfry in a little oil, about 3 to 5 minutes per side until golden and crispy, or bake at 350°F (180°C, or gas mark 4) for 15 minutes per side, covered loosely in foil, until firm and warmed all the way through, or grill. If you grill, wrap in foil to avoid having them fall apart, for about 20 minutes, until firm and warmed all the way through.

YIELD: 8 BURGERS

Mind Your Peas and 'Ques

48

Yeah, I know, one doesn't normally think of peas and barbecue sauce together, but believe me when I tell you that it really works!

INGREDIENTS:

¾ cup (180 ml) vegetable broth

½ cup (136 g) barbecue sauce, store-bought or homemade (page 183)

1 yellow onion, diced

2 cloves garlic, minced

2 tablespoons (30 g) horseradish

2 tablespoons (30 g) Dijon mustard

1 tablespoon (6 g) freshly ground black pepper

1 pound (454 g) fresh or frozen peas

¼ cup (60 ml) olive oil

1 cup (144 g) vital wheat gluten flour

½ cup (60 g) whole wheat flour

Salt

Oil, for frying (optional)

DIRECTIONS:

In a stockpot, bring the broth and barbecue sauce to a boil. Lower the heat to a simmer.

Add the onion and garlic, cover, and cook over medium-low heat for about 20 minutes, or until soft and most of the liquid has been absorbed.

Stir in the horseradish, mustard, pepper, and peas. Heat through. Transfer to a food processor or blender, or use an immersion blender to purée until smooth, but still a bit chunky.

Transfer to a mixing bowl. Stir in the olive oil. Let cool.

Slowly add the flours, season with salt, and knead until a nice patty-able consistency is reached.

Form into 4 to 6 patties and cook as desired.

Fry in oil until golden and crispy, 3 to 5 minutes per side. Alternatively, bake in the oven at 350°F (180°C, or gas mark 4), on a baking sheet lined with parchment paper or a silicone baking mat, loosely covered in foil, for 15 minutes, then flip and bake for 15 minutes longer, or until firm and warmed all the way through.

YIELD: 4 TO 6 BURGERS

SERVING SUGGESTION

Serve on a nice soft Plain White Bun (page 196) with Creamy BBQ Coleslaw (page 215) piled on top or on the side.

Super Quinoa Burger

WHEAT FREE **SOY FREE**

Since quinoa is the super grain, I shall dub these Super Burgers! These have a wonderful flavor, and I will surely admit to eating the mixture right from the bowl (minus the cornstarch) before I make the patties. In fact, it wouldn't make a bad side dish just as is. Plop a scoop on a plate next to a main dish and done.

INGREDIENTS:

1½ cups (355 ml) vegetable broth

1 cup (173 g) uncooked quinoa

1 can (15 ounces, or 420 g) cannellini or navy beans, rinsed and drained

2 cups (300 g) fresh or frozen green peas

½ cup (65 g) raw cashews, ground into a fine powder

1 teaspoon green curry paste

1 teaspoon ground ginger

2 tablespoons (32 g) tahini paste

2 tablespoons (30 ml) sesame oil

½ cup (64 g) cornstarch

Salt and pepper

Oil, for frying

DIRECTIONS:

Bring the vegetable broth to a boil.

Meanwhile, in a dry pan, heat the uncooked quinoa until it begins to pop (this will happen fairly quickly).

Add the quinoa to the broth, and lower the heat to medium. Cover and cook for 12 minutes, or until all of the broth is absorbed. Remove from the heat, fluff with a fork, and let sit, uncovered, to cool.

In a large mixing bowl, combine the beans, peas, cashews, curry, ginger, tahini, and oil. Gently mush the peas and beans, but don't completely mash; chunky is good.

When the quinoa is cooled, fold it into the mixture and add the cornstarch and salt and pepper to taste. Mix well using your hands.

Refrigerate for at least 20 minutes to thicken up a bit before forming into 8 patties.

Panfry in a smidge of oil in a pan until golden on each side, about 3 minutes per side.

These taste best panfried. The oven makes them too dry, and they won't hold up well on a grill.

YIELD: 8 BURGERS

SERVING SUGGESTION

I like buns, but this one really tastes good on lettuce. Red leaf is my favorite. A nice big leaf, topped with the patty, some alfalfa sprouts, and drizzled with Tangy Tahini Sauce (page 182, and pictured here). So yum. Brown rice makes a good side dish.

50 Mushroom Chicken Burger

WHEAT FREE

I don't know how much these actually taste like chicken, but they definitely have a "white meat" flavor to them that the other TVP burgers don't. You can use any vegetable broth in this recipe, but I like the "chicken-flavored broth powder" sold in the bulk bins at your local health-food store.

INGREDIENTS:

1 cup (96 g) TVP granules

1 cup (235 ml) vegetable broth

8 ounces (227 g) mushrooms, sliced or chopped to your desired size (I like mine chunky)

2 cloves garlic, minced

2 tablespoons (30 ml) olive oil

8 ounces (227 g) plain tempeh, crumbled into small bits

¼ cup (30 g) nutritional yeast

2 tablespoons (16 g) cornstarch

2½ tablespoons (19 g) ground flaxseed mixed with 3 tablespoons (45 ml) water

Salt and pepper

Oil, for frying (optional)

SERVING SUGGESTION

On a bun with vegan mayo (page 191) and tomatoes. These are very neutral in flavor, so you could pretty much dress them up any way you want!

DIRECTIONS:

In a microwave-safe bowl, mix together the TVP granules and the broth, cover tightly with plastic wrap, and microwave for 5 to 6 minutes. Alternatively, bring the broth to a boil, pour over the TVP granules, cover, and let sit for 10 minutes. Let cool.

In a pan, sauté the mushrooms and garlic in the oil for about 5 minutes, or until the mushrooms have reduced in size to about half.

Lower the heat, add the crumbled tempeh, and cook for 5 minutes longer, being careful not to burn. Let cool.

In a mixing bowl, combine the TVP with the mushroom mixture, nutritional yeast, cornstarch, flax mixture, and salt and pepper to taste. Knead very well, using your hands, to get it all smooshed and mooshed together.

Form into 5 or 6 patties and cook as desired.

I make these on the grill, individually wrapped loosely in foil, essentially steaming them. They stay very moist. They can also be panfried, microwaved, or baked.

To bake them, bake at 350°F (180°C, or gas mark 4) for 15 minutes on each side, loosely covered with foil to prevent them from drying out, until firm and heated all the way through.

YIELD: 5 OR 6 BURGERS

Crab Cakes

These are the prettiest patties! I make 'em small, and I fry them in a lot of oil. Kind of like crab cakes. I like how the carrots kind of imitate the look of crabmeat.

INGREDIENTS:

¼ cup (20 g) hijiki seaweed

2 cups (470 ml) hot water

12 ounces (340 g) extra-firm tofu, drained and pressed

1 can (15 ounces, or 420 g) chickpeas, drained and rinsed

1 yellow onion, diced

1 cup (108 g) shredded carrots

1 cup (144 g) vital wheat gluten flour

2 tablespoons (16 g) Old Bay Seasoning

Salt and pepper

½ cup (120 ml) soy or coconut milk (optional, for coating)

1 cup (80 g) panko bread crumbs (optional, for coating)

Oil, for frying

SERVING SUGGESTION

I don't serve these on a bun, although I'm sure they'd taste good that way. I just like to serve these on a bed of greens with Aioli Dipping Sauce (page 189).

DIRECTIONS:

Place the hijiki in the hot water and let sit for 10 minutes to reconstitute.

While it's soaking, in a mixing bowl, crumble the tofu, and then add the chickpeas, onion, carrots, flour, Old Bay, and salt and pepper to taste. Mix together with your hands, making sure that you mash some of the chickpeas while leaving some of them intact. Make sure, also, that the flour gets mixed in well and that there are no lumps.

Strain the hijiki, reserving the liquid. Add the hijiki to the mixture and mix well. If the mixture needs more moisture, add a little of the reserved hijiki water until you get a nice patty-able consistency.

Refrigerate for at least 20 minutes before forming into 15 crab cake–size patties. Refrigerate the patties for at least 2 to 3 hours before cooking so that the flavor of the hijiki gets well incorporated. Overnight is even better.

If desired, pour the soymilk into a shallow dish and spread the bread crumbs on a plate. Dip each patty into the soymilk, then dredge in the bread crumbs.

Panfry in oil for 3 to 4 minutes per side, until golden and crispy.

YIELD: 15 BURGERS

52 Sunday Afternoon Grillers

These burgers were designed to look like the "other" burgers on the grill when you go to a barbecue where those "other" burgers might be cooked. That's why they need a food processor to make. It gives them that real "ground beef" look. They smell so good that the carnies will be begging for one of yours instead. They hold together nicely on the grill, as long as you remember to oil either the grill or the burger so that they don't stick. If you are worried about sharing the grill with the carnies, you can always wrap yours in foil and cook them that way.

INGREDIENTS:

2 tablespoons (30 ml) vegetable oil

1 cup (96 g) TVP granules

1 cup (235 ml) vegetable broth or water

8 ounces (227 g) mushrooms, roughly chopped

1 white onion, roughly chopped

2 cloves garlic, roughly chopped

1 cup (144 g) vital wheat gluten flour

¼ cup (30 g) nutritional yeast

¼ cup (60 ml) tamari or soy sauce

6 ounces (170 g) tomato paste

1 cup (96 g) diced scallion

SERVING SUGGESTION

Serve with the traditional barbecue fare. Corn on the cob, baked beans, fries, macaroni or potato salad . . . As far as the fixins? Vegan mayo (page 191), ketchup, lettuce, tomato, onion, pickle . . .

DIRECTIONS:

Preheat the oil in a flat-bottomed skillet over medium-high heat.

In a microwave-safe bowl, mix together the TVP granules and the broth, cover tightly with plastic wrap, and microwave for 5 to 6 minutes. Alternatively, bring the broth to a boil, pour over the TVP granules, cover, and let sit for 10 minutes.

While the TVP is reconstituting, add the mushrooms, onion, and garlic to the pan. Sauté for 5 to 6 minutes, or until fragrant and beginning to brown.

In a food processor, combine the sautéed mushroom mixture, reconstituted TVP, gluten flour, nutritional yeast, tamari, and tomato paste. Process until well combined and "meaty" looking.

Transfer to a bowl and mix in the scallion. Form into 6 to 8 patties.

You can bake or fry these, but my favorite way to serve them is grilled.

Use a lower flame, oil the grill, and slow cook them for about 10 minutes per side. BE PATIENT! Don't flip them too early or they will stick, and you won't get those sought-after grill marks.

These also freeze well, so you can make them in advance and bring them to your next summertime get-together.

YIELD: 6 TO 8 BURGERS

53 Seitanic Stuffer

This is really four separate burgers! Yummy, "beefy" outer burgers with yummy, gooey surprises inside. Actually, you could probably make 101 versions of just this burger. Once you make the burger dough, you can pretty much stuff them with anything you want (the four Stuffer recipes that follow are my favorites).

FOR BURGER DOUGH:

2 cups (288 g) vital wheat gluten flour

1 cup (120 g) whole wheat flour

¼ cup (30 g) nutritional yeast

2 tablespoons (16 g) garlic powder

2 tablespoons (16 g) onion powder

2 tablespoons (4 g) dried parsley

1 teaspoon paprika

Salt and pepper (I like a lot of black pepper in mine!)

1 cup (235 ml) vegetable broth

⅔ cup (160 ml) Bragg's Liquid Aminos or soy sauce (if using regular soy sauce, use ⅓ cup [80 ml] soy sauce plus ⅓ cup [80 ml] water or vegetable broth)

⅓ cup (80 ml) olive oil

¼ cup (66 g) tomato paste

FOR FILLING:

Filling of your choice (pages 101-105)

DIRECTIONS:

Preheat the oven to 350°F (180°C, or gas mark 4). Line a baking sheet with parchment or a silicone baking mat.

In a large mixing bowl, combine the flours, nutritional yeast, garlic powder, onion powder, parsley, paprika, and salt and pepper to taste.

In a separate bowl, combine the broth, liquid aminos, oil, and tomato paste. Add the wet ingredients to the dry and knead vigorously for about 5 minutes. Let rest for about 20 minutes.

Form the dough into 12 patties and place on the prepared baking sheet. Scoop a good amount, about ¼ cup (65 g), of filling into the center of 6 of the patties. Sandwich the other 6 patties on top and pinch together the edges. Cover the baking sheet with foil to prevent them from drying out.

Bake for approximately 60 minutes, until firm.

YIELD: 6 BURGERS

SERVING SUGGESTION

No matter which stuffer you make, know that these fellas are whoppers (no pun intended), so make sure to keep the sides light and green if possible.

Smoky Tempeh Seitanic Stuffer

Oh! The smoky tender juiciness of this filling is the perfect way to introduce tempeh to those who might be just a little bit tempeh-timid.

FOR BURGER DOUGH:

1 recipe Seitanic Stuffer (page 100)

FOR FILLING:

8 ounces (227 g) plain soy tempeh, crumbled

1 cup (160 g) finely diced onion

¼ cup (30 g) nutritional yeast

3 tablespoons (54 g) white or yellow miso

3 tablespoons (18 g) imitation bacon bits, store-bought or homemade (page 185)

1 tablespoon (7 g) paprika

¼ teaspoon liquid smoke

Black pepper

DIRECTIONS:

Mix all the ingredients together until fully incorporated. Use as a filling for the Seitanic Stuffer dough (page 100).

SERVING SUGGESTION

Serve this savory burger on a hearty bun with minimal dressing . . . maybe a bit of vegan mayo (page 191). Serve alongside a big pile of steamed or sautéed greens like kale or collards to round out the meal.

55 Inside-Out Cheeseburger Seitanic Stuffer

This is the recipe for "Nutty Cheeze" from my first book, *Cozy Inside*. This recipe makes way more than you will need to stuff the burgers, but who doesn't need some extra yummy, sliceable cheeze in the fridge?

FOR BURGER DOUGH:

1 recipe Seitanic Stuffer (page 100)

FOR FILLING:

1 ounce (28 g) agar flakes or powder

3 cups (705 ml) water

2 cups (260 g) raw cashews, finely ground into a powder

3 tablespoons (45 ml) fresh lemon juice

2 tablespoons (30 ml) sesame oil

¼ cup (30 g) nutritional yeast

2 teaspoons (11 g) sea salt

½ teaspoon onion powder

½ teaspoon garlic powder

DIRECTIONS:

Spray a loaf pan with nonstick spray and set aside.

In a stockpot, combine the agar and the water and bring to a full boil; boil for 5 minutes. Whisk regularly.

In a food processor, combine the cashew powder, lemon juice, sesame oil, nutritional yeast, salt, onion powder, and garlic powder, and blend until well incorporated.

Pour into the water-agar mixture and mix until creamy and smooth; remove from the heat.

Pour into the prepared loaf pan and refrigerate for at least 1 hour, or until hardened.

Use as a filling for the Seitanic Stuffer dough (page 100).

SERVING SUGGESTION

Dress as you would any cheeseburger. This one tastes especially great on thick slices of grilled sour dough. Serve up with a nice, crisp garden salad.

RECIPE NOTE

You can make several variations from adding fresh herbs and spices to the mix. When I want a Mediterranean cheese, I add sun-dried tomatoes and fresh basil. When I want a Mexican cheese, I add cumin and chopped jalapeños. If I want a smoky cheese, I add a little bit of liquid smoke. It's limitless!

Spanakopita-ish Seitanic Stuffer

This makes more filling than you will need for the burgers, so feel free to cut the recipe in half. Or make the whole thing and use the leftovers inside phyllo triangles or inside a tortilla for a quick and easy wrap for lunch.

FOR BURGER DOUGH:

1 recipe Seitanic Stuffer (page 100)

FOR FILLING:

14 ounces (392 g) extra-firm tofu, drained, pressed, and crumbled

1 can (14 ounces, or 392 g) spinach, drained, or 2 cups (60 g) fresh spinach leaves, cut into chiffonade

½ cup (80 g) finely diced white or yellow onion

⅓ cup (40 g) pine nuts

⅓ cup (37 g) finely chopped sun-dried tomatoes

¼ cup (30 g) nutritional yeast

2 tablespoons (16 g) garlic powder

1 tablespoon (15 ml) lemon juice

Salt and pepper

DIRECTIONS:

In a bowl, combine all the ingredients. Mix until well incorporated. Using your hands yields the best results. Refrigerate until ready to use. Use as a filling for the Seitanic Stuffer dough (page 100).

SERVING SUGGESTION

Keep the Greek theme going by spreading a little hummus on a toasty bun before serving. Top the whole thing off with a few Kalamata olives skewered on a toothpick.

Garlic, Mushroom, and Onion Seitanic Stuffer

I love this classic combo of ingredients. Not only does this filling work smashingly for the Seitanic Stuffer, but it also works well in phyllo triangles, samosas, and puff pastry.

FOR BURGER DOUGH:

1 recipe Seitanic Stuffer (page 100)

FOR FILLING:

1 cup (160 g) diced onion

8 ounces (227 g) mushrooms, sliced

2 tablespoons (30 g) minced garlic

2 tablespoons (30 ml) olive oil

½ cup (120 ml) vegetable broth

¼ cup (60 ml) soy sauce

2 tablespoons (16 g) all-purpose flour

DIRECTIONS:

In a skillet or frying pan, sauté the onion, mushrooms, and garlic in the oil over medium-high heat until the mushrooms have reduced in volume by about half, 5 to 7 minutes.

Add the vegetable broth and soy sauce and bring to a simmer. Reduce the heat to low.

Sprinkle in the flour and knead until thickened. Use as a filling for the Seitanic Stuffer dough (page 100).

SERVING SUGGESTION

Serve on a toasted onion bun spread with Simple Pesto (page 186) and topped with fresh, juicy slices of yellow or red tomatoes. Let the burger be the star and keep the sides simple—and what could be simpler than a handful of chips?

58 BLT and Avocado Burger

Let me start off by saying that there is an INSANE amount of imitation bacon bits in this recipe. Seriously, though, what's a BLT without a ton of bacon?

INGREDIENTS:

1 cup (144 g) vital wheat gluten flour

1 cup (125 g) all-purpose flour

1 cup (80 g) imitation bacon bits, store-bought or homemade (page 185)

1 tablespoon (8 g) garlic powder

1 tablespoon (8 g) onion powder

½ teaspoon ground black pepper

1 cup (180 g) diced tomatoes

¼ cup (60 ml) vegetable oil

2 tablespoons (30 ml) steak sauce

2 tablespoons (30 g) ketchup

2 ripe avocados

DIRECTIONS:

In a large bowl, combine the flours, bacon bits, garlic powder, onion powder, and pepper.

In a separate bowl, mix together the tomatoes, oil, steak sauce, and ketchup.

Add the wet ingredients to the dry and knead together until uniformly mixed. Let sit for 20 minutes.

Preheat the oven to 350°F (180°C, or gas mark 4). Line a baking sheet with parchment or a silicone baking mat.

Divide the mixture into 8 equal pieces, and flatten each piece.

Place ½ avocado, mushed, into the center of 4 of the flattened pieces.

Sandwich with the remaining 4 pieces and pinch the edges to seal.

Bake, covered in foil, for 20 minutes, then flip and bake for 15 minutes longer, or until firm

YIELD: 4 HUGE BURGERS

SERVING SUGGESTION

Serve on a toasted sourdough bun with a schmear of vegan mayo (page 191) and, of course, a thick tomato slice and a nice leaf of crispy lettuce. Feel free to throw some bacon bits on top for good measure!

59 Confetti Burger

WHEAT FREE **SOY FREE**

The bright colors in this patty remind me of a party, hence the name *confetti*.

INGREDIENTS:

1 cup (225 g) dried split peas

1 cup (192 g) dried lentils

4 cups (940 ml) vegetable broth

2 tablespoons (30 ml) olive oil

2 cups (298 g) diced red, yellow, and green bell peppers

1 cup (160 g) diced red onion

2 tablespoons (30 g) minced garlic

2 tablespoons (33 g) tomato paste

1 teaspoon curry powder

1 teaspoon chipotle powder

¼ cup (64 g) tahini

2 tablespoons (30 ml) sesame oil

½ cup (122 g) unsweetened applesauce

Salt and pepper

2 cups (114 g) instant potato flakes

Oil, for frying (optional)

SERVING SUGGESTION

Enjoy this festive little guy on a toasted gluten-free bun schmeared with Aioli Dipping Sauce (page 189) alongside some Sweet Potato Fries (page 206).

DIRECTIONS:

In a large stockpot, combine the peas, lentils, and broth and bring to a boil. Boil hard for 4 minutes. Reduce to a simmer, cover, and simmer until tender. Depending on the age of the beans, it could take as little as 10 minutes or as long as an hour, so keep a watchful eye. Drain.

While the peas and lentils are cooking, preheat the olive oil in a flat skillet over medium-high heat. Add the peppers and onion and sauté until tender, 5 to 7 minutes.

Add the garlic, and cook for 2 to 3 minutes longer. Remove from the heat and transfer to a large mixing bowl, along with the fully cooked and drained lentils and peas. Let cool.

Add the tomato paste, curry powder, chipotle powder, tahini, sesame oil, applesauce, and salt and pepper to taste. Mash together until well incorporated.

Begin adding the potato flakes a little bit at a time, kneading until you get a nice patty-able consistency.

Form into 10 to 12 patties and cook as desired.

Bake, covered in foil, at 350°F (180°C, or gas mark 4) for 15 minutes, then flip and bake for 15 minutes longer, until firm, or panfry in oil for 3 to 5 minutes per side until a golden crust forms.

YIELD: 10 TO 12 BURGERS

The Crunch and Munch Burger

60

It's the crunch that keeps you coming back for more munch!

INGREDIENTS:

2 tablespoons (30 ml) olive oil

8 ounces (227 g) mushrooms, sliced or chopped

3 cloves garlic, minced

¾ cup (180 ml) vegetable broth

1 cup (96 g) TVP granules

2 stalks celery, diced

¼ cup (27 g) shredded carrot

1 cup (70 g) shredded red or green cabbage

½ cup (65 g) cashews (raw or roasted is fine)

½ cup (72 g) vital wheat gluten flour, plus more if needed

¼ cup (60 g) nondairy sour cream, store-bought or homemade (page 191)

2 tablespoons (30 g) sweet pickle relish

1 tablespoon (8 g) ground mustard

1 tablespoon (8 g) onion powder

Salt and pepper

Oil, for frying

DIRECTIONS:

In a heavy-bottom skillet, heat the oil and sauté the mushrooms and garlic for 5 to 7 minutes, or until fragrant and translucent.

Add the vegetable stock and bring to a simmer.

Add the TVP granules, mix well, cover, and remove from the heat. Let sit for 10 minutes.

When cool enough to handle, add the celery, carrot, cabbage, cashews, flour, sour cream, relish, mustard, onion powder, and salt and pepper to taste, and mix well using your hands, adding more flour, a little bit at a time, if the dough is too sticky.

Place in the fridge to cool for about 20 minutes and help stiffen the dough.

Form into 4 patties.

These are best fried in a skillet with a little oil for 4 to 5 minutes per side, or until a nice crispy crust forms.

YIELD: 4 BURGERS

SERVING SUGGESTION

The burger itself has so much crunch that it's best with a soft Sweet Potato Bun (page 201) and a dollop of vegan mayo (page 191).

The Trifecta Burger

61

The three *T*s of soy (TVP, Tofu, and Tempeh) join forces to create a protein-packed burger that will rock your socks off.

INGREDIENTS:

1 cup (96 g) TVP granules

1 cup (235 ml) vegetable broth

10 ounces (280 g) extra-firm tofu, drained and pressed

4 ounces (112 g) plain soy tempeh

½ cup (112 g) vegan mayonnaise, store-bought or homemade (page 191)

2 tablespoons (34 g) Sriracha sauce

2 tablespoons (30 ml) sesame oil

½ cup (62 g) all-purpose flour

Oil, for frying (optional)

DIRECTIONS:

In a microwave-safe bowl, mix together the TVP granules and the broth, cover tightly with plastic wrap, and microwave for 5 to 6 minutes. Alternatively, bring the broth to a boil, pour over the TVP granules, cover, and let sit for 10 minutes. Let cool.

In a mixing bowl, crumble the tofu and tempeh. Mix in the reconstituted TVP.

Add the mayonnaise, Sriracha sauce, and sesame oil. Mix well.

Slowly knead in the flour until well incorporated and form into 6 patties. Cook as desired.

Bake at 350°F (180°C, or gas mark 4) for 30 minutes, flipping halfway through, or bake first, then finish off by lightly frying in a smidge of oil until golden and crispy, 2 to 3 minutes on each side.

YIELD: 6 BURGERS

SERVING SUGGESTION

Serve on a toasted bagel or toasted white bun with a generous schmear of Tangy Tahini Sauce (page 182), lettuce, tomato, and sprouts, as pictured. A big helping of steamed veggies would also complement this nicely.

62 Meatloaf Burger

Growing up, the best thing about meatloaf for dinner was meatloaf sandwiches for lunch the next day! These burgers make "leftovers" without having to make dinner first!

INGREDIENTS:

3 cups (288 g) TVP granules

2½ cups (590 ml) vegetable broth or water

2 tablespoons (30 ml) soy sauce or tamari

2 tablespoons (30 ml) olive oil

1 large yellow onion, finely diced

2 cloves garlic, minced

1 teaspoon ground black pepper

1 tablespoon (8 g) garlic powder

1 tablespoon (8 g) onion powder

½ teaspoon cumin

1 cup (240 g) ketchup or barbecue sauce, store-bought or homemade (page 183), plus extra for basting

1½ cups (216 g) vital wheat gluten flour

SERVING SUGGESTION

I like these on a toasted white roll with the usual burger fixin's: a schmear of vegan mayo (page 191), a thick slice of onion, a pickle, some greens, a tomato slice, and a nice big dollop of ketchup. If serving for dinner, mashed potatoes are a perfect side.

DIRECTIONS:

Preheat the oven to 350°F (180°C, or gas mark 4). Line a baking sheet with parchment or a silicone baking mat.

In a microwave-safe bowl, mix together the TVP granules, broth, and soy sauce, cover tightly with plastic wrap, and microwave for 5 to 6 minutes. Alternatively, bring the broth and soy sauce to a boil, pour over the TVP granules, cover, and let stand for 10 minutes. Set aside to cool.

In a skillet, heat the olive oil and sauté the onion and garlic until translucent and just beginning to brown, 7 to 10 minutes.

Add to the reconstituted TVP, along with the pepper, garlic powder, onion powder, cumin, 1 cup (240 g) ketchup, and flour. Mix well. Use your hands and knead the mixture together. Make sure everything is well incorporated. Let the mixture sit for at least 20 minutes, to let the gluten develop.

Form into 8 patties and place on the prepared baking sheet.

Bake, uncovered, for 15 minutes.

Remove from the oven and brush with the additional ketchup, return to the oven, and bake for 15 minutes longer, or until firm and the ketchup begins to turn a dark caramelized crimson.

YIELD: 8 BURGERS

63 Tofu 'n' Roots Burger

Bulb fennel is such an underused and underrated ingredient. The sweet savory combos that it can handle are simply limitless.

INGREDIENTS:

2 tablespoons (28 g) nondairy butter

1 bulb (5 to 6 ounces, or 140 to 168 g) fennel, roughly chopped

1 onion, roughly chopped

12 ounces (340 g) sweet potatoes, peeled and cubed

2 cloves garlic, chopped

Pinch of salt

2 cups (470 ml) water

1 cup (96 g) TVP granules

1 teaspoon cumin

18 ounces (504 g) extra-firm tofu, drained and pressed

½ cup (72 g) vital wheat gluten flour

1 cup (125 g) all-purpose flour

Oil, for frying (optional)

SERVING SUGGESTION

This burger has a mellow, slightly sweet flavor. I like to complement this with some spicy Chipotle Dipping Sauce (page 184) on a toasted bun with a thick slice of red onion. A green side, such as steamed kale, broccoli, or asparagus, would work beautifully here.

DIRECTIONS:

Preheat the oven to 350°F (180°C, or gas mark 4). Line a baking sheet with parchment or a silicone baking mat.

In a frying pan or skillet, melt the butter over medium-high heat. Add the fennel, onion, sweet potatoes, and garlic. Sprinkle with a pinch of salt. Sauté until just beginning to brown, about 5 minutes.

Add the water, deglaze the pan, and bring to a boil. Lower the heat to a simmer, cover, and simmer for 15 minutes.

Stir in the TVP granules and cumin. Remove from the heat, cover, and let sit for 10 minutes.

Transfer to a large mixing bowl and crumble in the tofu, then add the flours. Knead with your hands until very well incorporated. Let sit for at least 20 minutes to thicken a bit.

Form into 8 to 10 patties and place on the prepared baking sheet.

Bake, uncovered, for 30 minutes, or bake for 20 minutes and finish off by panfrying in oil for about 3 minutes per side.

YIELD: 8 TO 10 BURGERS

Summer Squash Burger

These patties make a great breakfast, lunch, or dinner, depending on how you serve them.

INGREDIENTS:

1 cup (124 g) shredded yellow zucchini

1 cup (124 g) shredded green zucchini

2 cups (250 g) all-purpose flour

6 ounces (170 g) plain soy or other nondairy yogurt

¼ cup (60 ml) canola oil, plus more for frying

¼ cup (60 ml) soy or other nondairy milk

¼ teaspoon paprika

Salt and pepper

Oil, for frying

DIRECTIONS:

In a mixing bowl, combine the zucchinis, flour, yogurt, ¼ cup (60 ml) canola oil, milk, paprika, and salt and pepper to taste, mashing it together with your hands until you get a nice uniform mixture.

Form into 4 patties. Line a plate with paper towels.

Preheat ¼ inch (6 mm) oil in a frying pan over medium-high heat. The oil is ready when a piece of dough dropped into it sizzles immediately. Carefully add the patties, and fry for 3 to 4 minutes per side, until golden and crispy.

Transfer to the plate to absorb the excess oil.

YIELD: 4 BURGERS

RECIPE NOTE

Instead of making burgers, try making mini patties. Serve them as a side dish alongside your favorite protein.

SERVING SUGGESTION

For breakfast, serve this bunless alongside a tofu scramble. For lunch, serve this patty on whole wheat toast with a schmear of vegan mayo (page 191) and avocado. For dinner, serve on a crusty bun with a side of beans or potato salad.

Split Peas with Ham-burger

SOY FREE

It's like cramming a big bowl of split pea soup with chunks of ham into a burger! Booya!

FOR "HAM":

½ cup (60 g) chickpea flour

½ cup (72 g) vital wheat gluten flour

½ cup (120 ml) water or vegetable broth

¼ cup (60 ml) canola or vegetable oil

2 tablespoons (28 g) brown sugar

2 tablespoons (15 g) nutritional yeast

1½ tablespoons (25 g) tomato paste

½ teaspoon liquid smoke

½ teaspoon black pepper

¼ teaspoon salt

FOR BURGERS:

4 cups (940 ml) vegetable broth

2 cups (450 g) dried split peas

½ cup (62 g) all-purpose flour

½ cup (120 ml) canola oil, plus more for frying

2 tablespoons (16 g) onion powder

Salt and pepper

SERVING SUGGESTION

Serve this on a nice crusty piece of toasted sourdough or French bread. On the side? Perhaps some steamed cauliflower, drenched in a noochy cheezy sauce.

DIRECTIONS:

To make the "Ham": Preheat the oven to 350°F (180°C, or gas mark 4).

In a mixing bowl, mix together all the "Ham" ingredients until a nice goopy mixture forms.

Spread a large sheet of aluminum foil on the counter. Plop the mixture into the middle of the foil. Roll the foil over the mixture, and twist the ends tight, so that a nice log is formed. Place on a baking sheet, seam side down, and bake for about 45 minutes, or until firm. Remove from the oven and let cool.

Slice off a piece for yourself to snack on while you are cooking the split peas. Chop up the remaining "Ham" into ½-inch (1.3 cm) cubes for the burgers.

To make the burgers: In a pot, combine the broth and split peas. Cover and bring to a boil. Lower the heat to a simmer, and cook for 15 minutes longer.

Remove the lid, and continue cooking until tender and most of the liquid is absorbed, 5 to 7 minutes longer.

Transfer 3 cups (596 g) prepared peas to a mixing bowl and let cool.

Add the chopped "Ham," flour, the ½ cup (120 ml) oil, onion powder, and salt and pepper to taste, and knead with your hands. Form into 8 patties. Panfry in oil over medium-high heat for 3 to 5 minutes per side.

Although these taste best fried, they can also be baked at 350°F (180°C, or gas mark 4) for 15 minutes per side, loosely covered in foil, until firm and warmed all the way through.

YIELD: 8 BURGERS

66 Noochy Burger

This burger was made for the love of the nooch!

INGREDIENTS:

1 cup (96 g) TVP granules

1 cup (235 ml) vegetable broth

½ cup (128 g) cashew nut butter

¼ cup (64 g) tahini paste

½ cup (120 g) nondairy sour cream, store-bought or homemade (page 191)

2 tablespoons (36 g) white or yellow miso

½ cup (60 g) nutritional yeast

1 cup (144 g) vital wheat gluten flour

1 tablespoon (8 g) garlic powder

1 tablespoon (8 g) onion powder

1 tablespoon (7 g) paprika

¼ teaspoon turmeric

1 teaspoon (2 g) dried parsley or 1 tablespoon (4 g) chopped fresh parsley

Salt and pepper

Oil, for frying (optional)

DIRECTIONS:

In a microwave-safe bowl, mix together the TVP granules and broth, cover tightly with plastic wrap, and microwave for 5 to 6 minutes. Alternatively, bring the broth to a boil, pour over the TVP granules and cover. Let sit for 10 minutes until cool.

In a mixing bowl, combine the nut butter, tahini, sour cream, and miso. Add the reconstituted TVP and mix well.

In a separate bowl, combine the nutritional yeast, flour, garlic powder, onion powder, paprika, turmeric, parsley, and salt and pepper to taste.

Add the dry ingredients to the wet and knead together until a nice dough forms.

Form into 6 patties and cook as desired.

Fry in oil until golden and crispy, 3 to 5 minutes per side, or bake in the oven at 350°F (180°C, or gas mark 4), on a baking sheet lined with parchment or a silicone baking mat, loosely covered in foil, for 15 minutes, then flip and bake for 15 minutes longer, until firm and warmed all the way through.

YIELD: 6 BURGERS

SERVING SUGGESTION

I like to keep the fixin's simple on this one because the taste of this patty is pretty rich: a little vegan mayo (page 191), maybe some avocado and some ketchup, if you must, on a soft white sesame seed bun.

Burger Roll-ups

Otherwise known as a roulade, this dough is sliced and eaten as burgers. One roll yields 10 to 12 burgers, so there's plenty left over for work lunches and quick weeknight heat-ups.

FOR SEITAN DOUGH:

2 cups (288 g) vital wheat gluten flour

1 cup (120 g) whole wheat flour

½ cup (60 g) nutritional yeast

2 tablespoons (16 g) vegetable broth powder

2 tablespoons (16 g) garlic powder

2 tablespoons (16 g) onion powder

½ teaspoon paprika

Salt and pepper

2 cups (470 ml) water

½ cup (120 ml) olive oil

FOR FILLING:

8 ounces (227 g) extra-firm tofu, drained, pressed, and crumbled

3 tablespoons (45 g) nondairy cream cheese

2 tablespoons (16 g) ground raw cashews

2 tablespoons (15 g) pine nuts

1 cup (180 g) diced tomatoes, drained

1 cup (227 g) canned or frozen spinach, drained

½ cup (80 g) diced onion

2 tablespoons (15 g) nutritional yeast

1 tablespoon (15 g) minced garlic

DIRECTIONS:

To make the seitan dough: In a mixing bowl, combine the flours, nutritional yeast, vegetable broth powder, garlic powder, onion powder, paprika, and salt and pepper to taste. Add water and oil and knead for about 5 minutes. Cover and let sit for 20 minutes.

Preheat the oven to 350°F (180°C, or gas mark 4). Line a baking sheet with parchment or a silicone baking mat.

To make the filling: Mush all the filling ingredients together in a bowl and set aside until ready to use.

Next, roll out the dough into a large rectangle. Transfer to the prepared baking sheet and bake, uncovered, for 20 minutes.

Remove from the oven (do not turn off the oven) and spread on the filling to about 1 inch (2.5 cm) from the edges. Roll up tightly and place seam side down on a large sheet of aluminum foil, roll up, and twist the edges tight. Place on the baking sheet and bake for 60 to 70 minutes, until firm. Remove from the oven and let sit until cool enough to handle.

Unwrap and cut into 10 to 12 slices, ½ to ¾ inch (1.3 to 1.9 cm) thick, and serve on your favorite bun.

YIELD: 10 TO 12 BURGERS

SERVING SUGGESTION

Serve on a Sweet Potato Bun (page 201) with vegan mayo (page 191).

CHAPTER 7

BURGERS WITH LATIN FLAVOR

SPICY AND SASSY BURGERS INSPIRED BY THE AMIGOS AND AMIGAS I HAVE COME TO KNOW AND LOVE

68 Ortega Burger

These only take about 10 minutes to make, are loaded with protein, are super low in fat and carbs, but are super high in flavor!

INGREDIENTS:

1 cup (96 g) TVP granules

1 scant cup (225 ml) water

2 tablespoons (16 g) taco seasoning, store-bought or homemade (page 184)

½ cup (72 g) vital wheat gluten flour

½ cup (80 g) your favorite salsa*

1 tablespoon (15 ml) hot sauce

Oil, for frying (optional)

If your salsa is really juicy, you might have to add a little extra flour.

SERVING SUGGESTION

Garnish with grilled Ortega chiles, onions, jalapeño, nondairy sour cream, salsa, and avocado. Serve with tortilla chips, guacamole, and salsa on the side.

DIRECTIONS:

In a microwave-safe bowl, mix together the TVP granules and the water, cover tightly with plastic wrap, and microwave for 5 to 6 minutes. Alternatively, bring the water to a boil, pour over the TVP granules, cover, and let sit for 10 minutes. Let cool.

Mix in the taco seasoning, then mix in the flour, salsa, and hot sauce. Let sit for about 20 minutes or refrigerate until ready to serve.

Form into 4 patties. Cook as desired.

These can be baked at 350°F (180°C, or gas mark 4), uncovered, for about 15 minutes per side, or until just crisp on the outside; fried, in oil or nonstick spray, for 3 to 5 minutes per side, until golden and crispy; or grilled. If grilling, wrap in foil so they don't fall apart.

YIELD: 4 BURGERS

Jalapeño Cornbread Burger

Cornbread meets burger, and it's getting pretty spicy.

INGREDIENTS:

1 cup (96 g) TVP granules

2 tablespoons (16 g) taco seasoning, store-bought or homemade (page 184)

1 tablespoon (8 g) cumin

1 scant cup (225 ml) water

1 cup (140 g) yellow cornmeal

16 to 20 slices jarred or canned jalapeños, diced

¼ cup (60 ml) juice from jar of jalapeños

¼ cup (60 ml) vegetable oil, plus more for frying (optional)

¼ cup (31 g) all-purpose flour

1 cup (160 g) diced white or yellow onion

½ cup (125 g) yellow corn kernels

¼ cup (40 g) diced red bell pepper (optional)

Salt and pepper

DIRECTIONS:

In a microwave-safe bowl, mix together the TVP granules, taco seasoning, cumin, and water. Cover tightly with plastic wrap and microwave for 5 to 6 minutes. Or, bring the water to a boil, pour over the TVP granules and spices, cover, and let sit for 10 minutes. Let cool.

Add the cornmeal, jalapeños, jalapeño juice, the ¼ cup (60 ml) oil, flour, onion, corn, bell pepper, and salt and pepper to taste. Knead thoroughly until all the cornmeal and flour are absorbed into the mix. Refrigerate for about 20 minutes.

Form into 6 patties and cook as desired.

To grill, wrap them loosely in foil and grill for about 20 minutes. It effectively steams itself inside the foil.

Or fry in oil until golden and crispy, 3 to 5 minutes per side, or bake in the oven at 350°F (180°C, or gas mark 4), on a baking sheet lined with parchment or a silicone baking mat, loosely covered in foil, for 25 to 30 minutes, flipping halfway through.

YIELD: 6 BURGERS

SERVING SUGGESTION

Garnish with Nacho Cheezy Sauce (page 182) and more jalapeños. Nondairy sour cream (page 191) is a nice garnish to cool it down a bit. Serve with a big bowl of chili.

70 Chipotle Sweet Potato Burger

Something about the sweetness of a sweet potato combined with the smoky spiciness of chipotle chiles has always reminded me of fall. For this burger, I didn't even need a bun to enjoy the savory with the sweet and just a hint of autumn peeking through.

INGREDIENTS:

1 large or 2 small sweet potatoes

1 can (7 ounces, or 195 g) chipotle chiles in adobo sauce, or less to taste

12 ounces (340 g) extra-firm tofu, drained, pressed, and crumbled

¼ cup (32 g) ground raw cashews

¼ cup (55 g) firmly packed brown sugar

½ teaspoon sea salt

Pinch of nutmeg

Pinch of cinnamon

½ to 1 cup (60 to 120 g) whole wheat pastry flour

SERVING SUGGESTION

Make the patties on the smallish side, and serve as an appetizer on a bed of greens with Chipotle Dipping Sauce (page 184).

DIRECTIONS:

Preheat the oven to 350°F (180°C, or gas mark 4).

Bake the sweet potatoes with the skin on, directly on the rack, for approximately 45 minutes, or until tender. Remove from the oven and let cool.

When cool, remove the skin (it should come right off) and smash the potato. Measure 2 cups (450 g) smashed sweet potato.

In a mixing bowl, place the potatoes, chipotles, tofu, ground cashews, brown sugar, salt, nutmeg, and cinnamon and mush together really well with your hands. The chipotles should break apart easily as you do this. After everything is well incorporated, add the flour, a little bit at a time.

Depending on the moisture content of your potato and tofu, you made need just a little or a lot. Refrigerate for 10 to 20 minutes.

Preheat the oven again to 350°F (180°C, or gas mark 4). Line a baking sheet with parchment or a silicone baking mat.

Form into 8 hearty patties and place on the prepared baking sheet.

Bake for 20 minutes, uncovered, then flip and bake for 20 minutes longer, until firm and just beginning to brown.

I like these better baked than fried.

YIELD: 8 BURGERS

71 Black Bean Tamale Burger with Mole Sauce WHEAT FREE SOY FREE

This burger can be baked, fried, or steam baked in cornhusks. The mole sauce is a simple version of a Mexican classic. You only need about 1 cup (240 g) for the actual burgers, so use the remainder to pour over them or mix in with rice. Serve the patty on its own or on a warm corn tortilla with Cilantro Lime Rice (page 216) and fajita-grilled vegetables.

FOR MOLE SAUCE:

1½ tablespoons (23 ml) vegetable oil

½ cup (80 g) finely diced white or yellow onion

1½ tablespoons (23 g) finely chopped garlic

½ teaspoon dried oregano

1 teaspoon cumin

¼ teaspoon cinnamon

2 tablespoons (16 g) chili powder, or to taste

2 ¼ cups (530 ml) vegetable broth

1 teaspoon (1 g) instant coffee crystals or 1 tablespoon (15 ml) brewed espresso

1 tablespoon (8 g) cornstarch dissolved in 2 tablespoons (30 ml) water to make a slurry

½ disc (0.75 ounce, or 21 g) Mexican or dark chocolate

FOR BURGERS:

3 cups (342 g) masa harina flour (I like Maseca brand)

1 cup (235 ml) oil

1 cup (235 ml) Mole Sauce (at right)

½ cup (120 ml) water

1 can (15 ounces, or 420 g) black or pinto beans, drained and rinsed

1 teaspoon cumin

1 teaspoon oregano

½ teaspoon cayenne pepper

Salt and pepper

Oil, for frying (optional)

10 large cornhusks, soaked in warm water for at least 1 hour (optional)

DIRECTIONS:

To make the mole sauce: Heat the oil in a skillet, add the onion and garlic, and sauté over medium heat until translucent, 5 to 7 minutes. Add the oregano, cumin, and cinnamon and cook for about 5 minutes longer.

Mix in the chili powder to taste, then slowly stir in the broth. Bring to a boil. Reduce the heat to a simmer.

Add the coffee crystals, or espresso, and cornstarch slurry, stir well, and continue to simmer until reduced and thickened, about 20 minutes.

Remove from the heat and stir in the chocolate until melted.

To make the burgers: In a mixing bowl, combine all the ingredients and knead until well incorporated.

Form into 8 patties and cook as desired.

Panfry in plenty of oil for 4 to 5 minutes per side, or until golden brown and crispy, or bake in the oven at 350°F (180°C, or gas mark 4), on a baking sheet lined with parchment or a silicone baking mat, covered in a foil tent, for about 10 minutes per side.

To steam bake in cornhusks, set aside 8 intact cornhusks and cut the remaining 2 cornhusks into strips. Take 1 intact cornhusk and place it on the counter with the pointy side facing away from you. Place the patty in the center of the husk. Fold the pointy end over the patty, toward you. Then fold each side of the remaining three sides of the husk over the patty and secure by tying with a strip of cornhusk. Repeat with the remaining 7 patties. Place seam side down on the baking sheet and bake in the oven at 350°F (180°C, or gas mark 4) for 20 minutes. No need to flip.

YIELD: 8 BURGERS

Sarah's Southwest Burger

This recipe yields eight whoppin' burgers, so unless you plan on feeding lots of hungry banditos, feel free to cut the recipe in half, or freeze the patties for quick dinners throughout the week.

INGREDIENTS:

1 cup (96 g) TVP granules

1 cup (235 ml) vegetable broth or water

1 can (15 ounces, or 420 g) black beans, drained

2 cups (280 g) canned, fresh, or frozen corn kernels

2 cups (330 g) cooked brown rice

1 heaping cup (190 g) diced tomatoes, drained

½ cup (80 g) finely diced onion

¼ cup (40 g) finely diced jarred jalapeños (optional)

3 tablespoons (45 ml) canola oil

1 cup (144 g) vital wheat gluten flour

¼ cup (32 g) cornstarch

2 tablespoons (16 g) garlic powder

2 tablespoons (16 g) onion powder

1 teaspoon unsweetened cocoa powder

1 teaspoon paprika

Salt and pepper

DIRECTIONS:

In a microwave-safe bowl, mix together the TVP granules and broth, cover tightly with plastic wrap, and microwave for 5 to 6 minutes. Alternatively, bring the broth to a boil, pour over the TVP granules, cover, and let sit for 10 minutes. Let cool.

In a mixing bowl, combine the beans, corn, cooked rice, tomatoes, onion, jalapeños, and oil.

In a separate bowl, mix together the flour, cornstarch, garlic powder, onion powder, cocoa, paprika, and salt and pepper to taste.

When cool enough to handle, combine the reconstituted TVP with the rice and veggie mixture. Mix well with your hands so that the beans and rice start to get mushed in pretty well with the TVP.

Add the flour and spice mixture, and knead for a few minutes until a nice dough forms. Place the mixture in the refrigerator for at least 30 minutes to rest.

Preheat the oven to 350°F (180°C, or gas mark 4). Line a baking sheet with parchment or a silicone baking mat.

Form into 8 patties, place on the prepared baking sheet, and bake, uncovered, for 15 minutes, then flip and bake for 15 minutes longer, until firm and just beginning to brown.

YIELD: 8 BURGERS

SERVING SUGGESTION

Serve on a nice hearty bun with a schmear of nondairy sour cream (page 191), avocado, and some salsa. Serve with tortilla chips and Cilantro Lime Rice (page 216).

Enchilada Burger

WHEAT FREE

Way less fattening and way less work than traditional enchiladas!

INGREDIENTS:

2 cups (470 ml) enchilada sauce

1 cup (160 g) diced onion

1 cup (96 g) TVP granules

⅓ cup (46 g) chopped black olives

¼ cup (24 g) diced scallion

1 cup (114 g) masa harina flour (I like Maseca brand)

½ cup (120 g) nondairy sour cream, store-bought or homemade (page 191)

5 slices jarred jalapeños, chopped

Oil, for frying (optional)

DIRECTIONS:

In a large stockpot, bring the enchilada sauce and diced onion to a boil.

Stir in the TVP granules. Remove from the heat, cover, and let sit for 10 minutes.

Add the olives, scallion, flour, sour cream, and jalapeños and knead until everything is well incorporated.

Form into 6 patties. Cook as desired. It's good both ways!

Panfry in oil for 3 to 5 minutes per side, or until golden brown and crispy, or bake in the oven at 350°F (180°C, or gas mark 4), on a baking sheet lined with parchment or a silicone baking mat, for about 15 minutes per side, until firm and just beginning to brown.

YIELD: 6 BURGERS

SERVING SUGGESTION

Serve topped with nondairy sour cream and extra scallions on a nice warm corn tortilla with some Cilantro Lime Rice (page 216).

74 Pintos and Rice Burger

SOY FREE

This one couldn't be simpler. Simply mush all the ingredients together and bake or fry. I'd be lying if I told you I didn't like it better fried, but baked tastes delicious too, and is certainly better for the waistline.

INGREDIENTS:

1 can (15 ounces, or 420 g) pinto beans, drained

2 cups (330 g) cooked brown or white rice

1 cup (180 g) diced tomatoes

1 cup (160 g) diced onion

½ cup (70 g) yellow cornmeal

½ cup (62 g) all-purpose flour

1 jalapeño pepper, seeded if desired, and diced

1 tablespoon (15 g) minced garlic

1 teaspoon hot sauce (I like Tabasco or Tapatío)

½ teaspoon ground cumin

Salt and pepper

Oil, for frying (optional)

DIRECTIONS:

In a mixing bowl, combine all the ingredients and knead with your hands.

Form into 8 patties and cook as desired.

Panfry in plenty of oil for 4 to 5 minutes per side, until golden and crispy, or bake, uncovered, at 350°F (180°C, or gas mark 4) for 15 minutes on a baking sheet lined with parchment or a silicone baking mat, then flip and bake for 15 minutes longer, until firm and just beginning to brown.

YIELD: 8 BURGERS

SERVING SUGGESTION

I like this one a couple of ways: as a burger, on a toasted bun smothered with guacamole and topped with a few slices of jalapeños; served up with a big old side of chips and salsa or a grilled ear of corn on the cob (as shown here); or sandwiched in a flour tortilla and grilled quesadilla style, with some Nacho Cheesy Sauce (page 182), guacamole, and nondairy sour cream.

75 "Travis Loves Cilantro" Burger

Travis is a good friend of mine. I have known him since grade school. When asked what he would like in a burger, he exclaimed, "CILANTRO! CILANTRO! CILANTRO!" And he wasn't talking about garnish. He wanted lots of the green stuff throughout the burger. So, cilantro haters beware, this one just screams with it.

INGREDIENTS:

1 cup (96 g) TVP granules

3 tablespoons (24 g) taco seasoning, store-bought or homemade (page 184)

1 cup (235 ml) water or vegetable broth

¼ cup (60 ml) canola oil

1 can (15 ounces, or 420 g) black or pinto beans, drained

1 bunch fresh cilantro, leaves chopped (stems discarded)

1 cup (144 g) vital wheat gluten flour

1 cup (125 g) all-purpose flour

¾ cup (180 g) nondairy sour cream, store-bought or homemade (page 191)

DIRECTIONS:

Preheat the oven to 350°F (180°C, or gas mark 4). Line a baking sheet with parchment or a silicone baking mat.

In a microwave-safe dish, combine the TVP granules and taco seasoning, and then add the water. Cover tightly with plastic wrap and microwave for 5 to 6 minutes. Alternatively, bring the water to a boil, pour over the TVP granules and taco seasoning, cover, and let sit for 10 minutes. Let cool.

Add the oil, beans, and cilantro and stir to combine.

Using your hands, knead in the flours until well incorporated.

Add the sour cream and knead again.

Form into 6 patties and place on the prepared baking sheet.

Bake, uncovered, for 15 to 20 minutes, then flip and bake for 15 minutes longer, until firm and just beginning to brown.

YIELD: 6 BURGERS

SERVING SUGGESTION

On a toasted bun topped with salsa or nondairy sour cream, avocado, and a thick juicy slice of red tomato. Serve with tortilla chips and salsa and a side of Cilantro Lime Rice (page 216) for a fiesta in your mouth.

Jalapeño Cheddar Burger

Not too spicy, but just enough kick to know it's there. The "cheddar" flavor comes from the miso and nutritional yeast.

INGREDIENTS:

1 cup (96 g) TVP granules

1 cup (235 ml) vegetable broth

¼ cup (30 g) nutritional yeast

1 teaspoon liquid smoke

12 slices jarred jalapeños, or to taste, diced

2 cloves garlic, minced

2 tablespoons (36 g) white or yellow miso

¼ cup (60 g) nondairy cream cheese

1 cup (144 g) vital wheat gluten flour

Oil, for frying (optional)

SERVING SUGGESTION

Serve on a toasted bun with a healthy dollop of Sweet Mustard Sauce (page 192) and a side of Cilantro Lime Rice (page 216).

DIRECTIONS:

In a microwave-safe dish, combine the TVP, vegetable broth, nutritional yeast, and liquid smoke. Cover tightly with plastic wrap and microwave for 5 to 6 minutes. Alternatively, bring the water to a boil, pour over the TVP granules, nutritional yeast, and liquid smoke, cover, and let sit for 10 minutes. Let cool.

Add the jalapeños, garlic, miso, cream cheese, and flour to the TVP mixture and knead together until a thick, well-blended dough is formed. Allow to rest for 20 minutes.

Form into 4 patties and cook as desired.

These taste great both fried and baked. They are also sturdy enough to grill, so have at it!

Panfry in oil over medium heat for 3 to 4 minutes per side, or until golden and crispy, or bake at 350°F (180°C, or gas mark 4), uncovered, on a baking sheet lined with parchment or a silicone baking mat, for 25 minutes, flipping halfway through.

To grill, find a spot on the grill over a medium-low flame, and cook for 5 to 7 minutes per side, remembering to add a little oil to the patties before placing them on the grill to ensure those pretty grill marks!

YIELD: 4 BURGERS

Three Bean Chili Burger

I love a big bowl of chili. This recipe starts with a nice chili recipe, and then whammo, turns it into a burger!

FOR CHILI:

1 can (15 ounces, or 420 g) pinto beans, with liquid

1 can (15 ounces, or 420 g) black beans, with liquid

1 can (15 ounces, or 420 g) red or kidney beans, with liquid

4 ounces (112 g) jarred jalapeño slices

6 ounces (170 g) tomato paste

1 tablespoon (6 g) black pepper

2 tablespoons (16 g) garlic powder

1 tablespoon (8 g) onion powder

1 tablespoon (8 g) chili powder

1 teaspoon ground cumin

1 cup (160 g) finely diced white or yellow onion

1 cup (235 ml) vegetable broth

Salt

1 cup (96 g) TVP granules

FOR BURGERS:

½ recipe Chili (above)

2 cups (240 g) masa harina flour (I like Maseca brand)

⅓ cup (80 ml) vegetable oil, plus more for frying (optional)

DIRECTIONS:

To make the chili: In a large stockpot, combine all the beans, jalapeño, tomato paste, pepper, garlic powder, onion powder, chili powder, cumin, onion, broth, and salt to taste. Mix well.

Bring to a boil, lower the heat to a simmer, cover, and let simmer for at least 20 minutes.

Uncover, stir in the TVP, remove from the heat, recover, and let sit for at least 10 minutes. Let cool. Divide the recipe in half and refrigerate one half for another use.

To make the burgers: In a large bowl, add the flour and the ⅓ cup (80 ml) oil to the reserved half of the Chili. Knead together well.

Form into 8 patties. Cook as desired.

To fry, panfry in oil over medium heat for about 5 minutes per side, or until a golden crispy crust forms. To bake, bake at 350°F (180°C, or gas mark 4) on a baking sheet lined with parchment or a silicone baking mat, lightly covered in foil to prevent drying out, for about 15 minutes per side, until firm and warmed all the way through.

YIELD: ABOUT 8 CUPS (2048 G) CHILI, OR 8 BURGERS

SERVING SUGGESTION

Serve open-faced with the remaining chili and all of your favorite chili toppers, such as nondairy sour cream (page 191, and pictured here), diced onion, guacamole, scallions, and, if it tickles your fancy, some Nacho Cheesy Sauce (page 182).

CHAPTER 8

BURGERS FROM AROUND THE WORLD

SINCE I COULDN'T COME UP WITH AN ENTIRE CHAPTER ON BURGERS FROM SLOVENIA . . .

78 Jamaican Jerk Burger

Spicy, spicy, spicy, yet strangely sweet! Traditional jerk uses Scotch bonnet chiles. These are a bit hard to find, and extremely hot! If you cannot find, or do not want to find, Scotch bonnets, you can reduce the heat a tad by using habaneros or jalapeños. But, even with jalapeños, these will be spicy. The jerk sauce can also be used to rub onto tofu or tempeh before baking or grilling.

FOR JERK SAUCE:

2 bunches (5 ounces, or 140 g) scallions, whites and light green parts only

¼ cup (32 g) ground allspice

¼ cup (60 ml) pineapple juice (from the can; see below)

8 cloves garlic

6 to 8 Scotch bonnet chiles, seeded and cored

1 tablespoon (8 g) ground thyme

1 teaspoon ground cinnamon

½ teaspoon ground nutmeg

½ teaspoon sea salt

½ teaspoon freshly ground black pepper

FOR BURGERS:

24 ounces (680 g) prepared seitan, store-bought or homemade (page 217), roughly chopped

1 white onion, roughly chopped

1 recipe Jerk Sauce (above)

8 pineapple rings, reserving the juice from the can

DIRECTIONS:

To make the jerk sauce: Place all the ingredients in a food processor and process until a paste forms. Transfer to a large bowl.

To make the burgers: Preheat the oven to 350°F (180°C, or gas mark 4). Line a baking sheet with parchment or a silicone baking mat.

In a food processor, combine the seitan and onion and process until crumbly.

Add to the Jerk Sauce paste and knead to combine.

Form into 8 patties and place on the prepared baking sheet. Place a pineapple ring on top of each patty before baking, if desired.

Bake, uncovered, for 45 minutes, until firm and browned.

YIELD: 2 CUPS (470 ML) SAUCE, 8 BURGERS

SERVING SUGGESTION

Serve on a soft white bun with a schmear of vegan mayo (page 191), topped with a grilled pineapple (or baked with the pineapple on top) and some Pineapple Orange Pomegranate Relish (page 192), as shown here.

79 Coconut Rum Rice Burger

WHEAT FREE **SOY FREE**

Inspired by the folks that enjoy a "seriously easygoing" lifestyle in Barbados. But don't let the innocent name fool you! This burger packs a spicy punch, so feel free to cut down the amount of Sriracha if you want the sweet flavors to poke through a bit more.

FOR RICE:

4 cups (940 ml) water

2 cups (360 g) uncooked jasmine rice

1 tablespoon (15 ml) white rice vinegar

1 tablespoon (21 g) agave nectar

¼ teaspoon salt

FOR BURGERS:

1 recipe Rice (above)

½ cup (120 ml) orange juice

1 cup (235 ml) coconut-flavored rum

½ cup (65 g) crushed macadamia nuts

1 tablespoon (15 g) minced garlic

1 cup (160 g) diced white onion

2 tablespoons (34 g) Sriracha sauce

1 cup (112 g) coconut flour

½ cup (120 ml) coconut oil, for frying

DIRECTIONS:

To make the rice: The easiest way is to throw all of those ingredients into a rice cooker and let it do the work. If you don't have a rice cooker, in a pot with a tight-fitting lid, bring the water to a boil. Add the rice, vinegar, agave, and salt. Stir, lower the heat to a simmer, cover, and cook for 20 to 25 minutes, or until the rice is tender and the liquid is absorbed. Stir occasionally to prevent scorching and sticking to the bottom of the pot.

Transfer the rice to a large mixing bowl and let cool.

To make the burgers: Combine the Rice and remaining burger ingredients and mix well.

Knead together until a patty-able consistency is reached. If necessary, add a little more flour.

Form into 8 to 10 patties.

Preheat a frying pan with the coconut oil over medium-high heat.

Panfry each burger for 3 to 5 minutes per side, or until a nice golden crispy crust forms.

YIELD: 8 TO 10 BURGERS

SERVING SUGGESTION

Serve with grilled pineapple rings and grilled bell peppers over a bed of crisp cabbage.

Ethiopian Berbere Patties

SOY FREE

80

The exotic spices and aromas here really take this burger to a whole new level. These are a bit labor-intensive, but man, they are so worth it.

FOR BERBERE SPICE MIXTURE:

2 teaspoons (4 g) whole cumin seeds

4 whole cloves

½ teaspoon black peppercorns

¼ teaspoon whole allspice

1 dried ancho chile, with seeds, ground into a powder

3 tablespoons (21 g) smoked paprika

1 teaspoon ground ginger

¼ teaspoon turmeric

¼ teaspoon ground cinnamon

1 teaspoon salt

FOR BURGERS:

1 cup (144 g) vital wheat gluten flour

2 cups (240 g) whole wheat flour

1 recipe Berbere Spice Mixture (above)

¼ cup (60 ml) olive oil

2 cups (470 ml) water

4 cups (940 ml) vegetable broth

2 tablespoons (16 g) all-purpose flour dissolved in ¼ cup (60 ml) water to make a slurry

DIRECTIONS:

To make the spice mixture: In a dry pan, toast the cumin seeds, cloves, peppercorns, and allspice for 1 to 2 minutes. Take care not to burn.

Grind the whole spices into a powder and add the chile powder, paprika, ginger, turmeric, cinnamon, and salt. Mix well.

To make the burgers: In a large mixing bowl, combine the flours and Berbere Spice Mixture.

Add the oil and water and knead for 5 straight minutes. Cover lightly with a dish towel and let sit for at least 30 minutes.

Form into 6 to 8 patties.

Bring the vegetable broth to a boil in a wide shallow pan (a cast-iron skillet works nicely here). Add the patties to the boiling broth in a single layer, being careful not to crowd the pan. You may have to do these in 2 batches.

Lower the heat to a simmer, cover, and simmer for 1 hour, checking to make sure the patties are not stuck to the bottom of the pan.

Remove the patties from the broth with a slotted spoon. Slowly add the flour slurry to the broth remaining in the pan and stir until thickened.

Serve the gravy in a dish for dipping.

YIELD: 6 TO 8 BURGERS

SERVING SUGGESTION

Serve open-faced with injera bread and a dish of gravy (see recipe at right) for dipping.

Aloha Teriyaki Burger

Take your tummy on a tropical vacation. My favorite getaway is Maui, and whenever I make these, I pretend I am sitting on the sandy white beach at Ka'anapali watching the locals dive off of Black Rock.

INGREDIENTS:

1 cup (96 g) TVP granules

¾ cup (180 ml) vegetable broth or water

2 tablespoons (30 ml) soy sauce

2 tablespoons (30 ml) teriyaki sauce, plus extra for frying

2½ tablespoons (19 g) ground flaxseed mixed with 3 tablespoons (45 ml) water

1 cup (155 g) crushed pineapple

2 tablespoons (28 g) brown sugar

½ cup (72 g) vital wheat gluten flour

½ cup (60 g) whole wheat flour

Salt and pepper

SERVING SUGGESTION

These are delicious on a grilled bun with lettuce, grilled Maui onions, and a thick, grilled pineapple ring.

DIRECTIONS:

In a microwave-safe bowl, combine the TVP, vegetable broth, soy sauce, and 2 tablespoons (30 ml) teriyaki. Cover tightly with plastic wrap and microwave for 5 to 6 minutes. Alternatively, bring the vegetable stock, soy sauce, and teriyaki to a boil in a pot, add to the TVP in a bowl, cover, and let stand for 10 minutes. Let cool.

Add the flax egg (the flaxseed and water mixture), pineapple, brown sugar, and flours. Season with salt and pepper to taste.

Mix well with your hands for about 5 minutes. The mixture should end up being a little sticky and stringy. Depending on the moisture level of your TVP and pineapple, you may need to add more or less flour.

Refrigerate for at least 20 minutes to thicken up a bit. Form into 6 patties.

In a nonstick pan or skillet, panfry the patties, adding more teriyaki sauce to taste. The teriyaki will caramelize and make a nice dark crust.

YIELD: 6 BURGERS

82 Kasha Burger

Kasha is a traditional porridge enjoyed in Eastern Europe. In Jewish cuisine, the addition of bow-tie pasta and brown gravy makes it kasha *varnishkes*. I thought bow ties were a little big for burgers, so I replaced them with couscous.

INGREDIENTS:

2 tablespoons (28 g) nondairy butter, plus extra for frying (optional)

½ cup (82 g) buckwheat groats (kasha)

1 onion, diced

2 cups (470 ml) vegetable broth

¾ cup (130 g) dried couscous

½ cup (60 g) rye flour

Salt and pepper

SERVING SUGGESTION

Serve this burger open-faced on grilled sourdough topped with brown gravy.

DIRECTIONS:

In a large skillet or pot, melt the 2 tablespoons (28 g) butter over medium heat. Add the buckwheat groats and cook for about 2 minutes, stirring constantly.

Add the onions and continue to cook and stir for about 5 minutes longer.

Add the broth. Bring to a boil, lower the heat to a simmer, cover, and cook for 10 minutes.

Stir in the couscous, remove from the heat, cover, and allow the couscous to absorb the moisture. Stir well and let cool.

Preheat the oven to 350°F (180°C, or gas mark 4). Line a baking sheet with parchment or a silicone baking mat.

Add the rye flour and salt and pepper to taste, and knead until a patty-able consistency is reached.

Form into 5 or 6 patties. Cook as desired.

Panfry in additional butter over medium heat for 3 to 4 minutes per side, or until golden and crispy, or bake at 350°F (180°C, or gas mark 4), uncovered, on a baking sheet lined with parchment or a silicone baking mat, for 10 minutes, then flip and bake for 10 minutes longer, until firm and just beginning to brown.

YIELD: 5 TO 6 BURGERS

Slovenian Fritaja Burger

83

Slovenia is a small European country that is bordered by Italy, Croatia, Hungary, Austria, and the Adriatic Sea. The cuisine in Slovenia is quite diverse. Because of the dramatic variations in climate and terrain throughout the different regions, the cuisine is influenced by many cultures. The fritaja is Slovenia and Croatia's answer to the Italian frittata, or a baked omelet.

INGREDIENTS:

1 bunch (about 18 stalks) asparagus, snapped at the natural break

2 tablespoons (30 ml) olive oil, plus extra for frying

2 tablespoons (30 g) minced garlic

1 cup (160 g) diced onion

12 ounces (340 g) extra-firm tofu, drained and pressed

1 tablespoon (8 g) vegetable broth powder

½ cup (72 g) vital wheat gluten flour

½ cup (62 g) all-purpose flour

Salt and pepper

1 cup (80 g) panko bread crumbs

SERVING SUGGESTION

Serve on its own, for breakfast or lunch, with a few slices of fresh tomato.

DIRECTIONS:

Bring a pot of salted water to a boil. Add the asparagus and boil for 15 minutes. Drain and set aside.

In a frying pan, heat the 2 tablespoons (30 ml) olive oil and sauté the garlic and onion until browned on all edges, about 7 minutes.

Crumble in the tofu, sprinkle in the broth powder, and continue to cook for about 5 minutes longer.

Carefully transfer the mixture to a food processor and add the cooked asparagus. Pulse until a uniform, but still slightly chunky, mixture forms.

Transfer to a mixing bowl.

Add the flours and salt and pepper to taste. Knead until well incorporated, lightly cover, and let sit for about 20 minutes.

Form into 6 patties. Line a plate with paper towels.

Preheat ¼ inch (6 mm) oil in a large frying pan over high heat. The oil is ready when a piece of dough dropped into it sizzles immediately.

Spread the panko in a shallow dish. Dredge the patties in the bread crumbs to coat, then fry for about 5 minutes per side, or until a dark, golden, crispy crust forms.

Transfer to the plate to drain the excess oil.

YIELD: 6 BURGERS

84 Quiche Lorraine Burger

WHEAT FREE

Delicieux pour le déjeuner ou à n'importe quel moment! Say what you will about the French, they know how to cook. *Bon appetit!*

INGREDIENTS:

1 cup (120 g) chickpea flour

8 ounces (227 g) plain soy tempeh, crumbled

½ cup (50 g) imitation bacon bits, store-bought or homemade (page 185)

½ cup (60 g) nutritional yeast

¼ cup (72 g) white or yellow miso

¼ cup (60 g) nondairy cream cheese

1 teaspoon black salt

Oil, for frying

DIRECTIONS:

In a large mixing bowl, knead all the ingredients together into a thick mass. Really get in there with your hands and mash it together. There is not a lot of moisture in the mixture, so you have to use a little elbow grease. It'll come together.

Form into 4 patties.

Panfry in oil for 3 to 5 minutes per side, or until a nice golden crispy crust forms.

YIELD: 4 BURGERS

SERVING SUGGESTION

If you didn't quite get the translation above, these are delicious for breakfast or anytime! Serve on a Bagel Bun (page 202) alongside some breakfast favorites, such as hash browns, and if you are really hungry, a nice tofu scramble. I also like to put a dollop of ketchup on mine.

RECIPE NOTE

Tempeh timid? Don't be afraid of the fermented good stuff. If you are new to tempeh, try simmering it in water or broth for about 20 minutes before using it in recipes to mellow the fermented flavor.

Chorizo and Egg Burger

WHEAT FREE

85

The first time I had a traditional Mexican breakfast was when I was about thirteen years old. I spent the night at my girlfriend Yvette's house and was served up beans and rice with tortillas. No forks. I was totally intrigued and obviously uneducated in the ways of Mexican culture. I've come a long way since then!

FOR MEXiMEET:

1 cup (96 g) TVP granules

2 tablespoons (14 g) paprika

1 teaspoon ground cumin

1 teaspoon sugar

1 teaspoon garlic powder

1 teaspoon onion powder

½ teaspoon cayenne pepper

½ teaspoon chili powder

½ teaspoon chipotle powder

½ teaspoon salt

1 cup (235 ml) water or vegetable broth

½ cup (120 ml) canola or other mild-flavored vegetable oil

FOR PATTiES:

2 tablespoons (30 ml) canola oil, plus extra for frying

1 cup (160 g) diced onion

1 tablespoon (8 g) mustard powder

½ teaspoon turmeric

1 teaspoon garlic powder

1 teaspoon onion powder

Salt and pepper

12 ounces (340 g) extra-firm tofu, drained and pressed

1 recipe MexiMeet (above)

½ cup (62 g) masa flour (I like Maseca brand)

DiRECTiONS:

To make the MexiMeet: In a microwave-safe bowl, mix together the TVP granules and the spices. Add the water, cover tightly with plastic wrap, and microwave for 5 to 6 minutes. Alternatively, bring the water to a boil, pour over the TVP granules and spices, cover, and let stand for 10 minutes. While still hot, carefully mix in the oil.

To make the patties: In a large, flat skillet, heat the 2 tablespoons (30 ml) oil over medium-high heat. Add the onion and sauté until just beginning to brown. Add the mustard powder, turmeric, garlic powder, onion powder, and salt and pepper to taste. Stir to combine.

Crumble in the tofu and continue to cook for about 5 more minutes. Remove from the heat. Stir in the MexiMeet and then the masa. Mix until crumbly and well incorporated. Let sit for about 20 minutes.

Form the mixture into 6 to 8 patties and panfry in additional oil for 3 to 5 minutes, or until a nice crispy crust forms.

YiELD: 6 TO 8 BURGERS

SERViNG SUGGESTiON

Serve with a side of frijoles and tortillas for an authentic Mexican breakfast. I like mine with some sour cream and a few slices of avocado (or guacamole). Use the MexiMeet as a taco or burrito filling, too!

86 Swedish Potato Dumpling Burger

This burger was inspired by a traditionally meat-filled Swedish potato dumpling. If you are a textural eater, you may find this one a little gummy, but I assure you, this is how it's supposed to be.

INGREDIENTS:

1½ pounds (682 g) russet potatoes, washed, peeled, and cut into chunks

2 cups (250 g) plus 2 tablespoons (16 g) all-purpose flour, divided

2 tablespoons (30 ml) oil

1 cup (160 g) diced onion

8 ounces (227 g) mushrooms, sliced

1 tablespoon (15 g) minced garlic

½ cup (120 ml) vegetable broth

1 tablespoon (15 ml) tamari or soy sauce

½ cup (67 g) fresh or frozen green peas

SERVING SUGGESTION

Serve bunless, topped with your favorite brown gravy, with a side of green beans.

DIRECTIONS:

Bring a large pot of salted water to a boil, add the potatoes, and boil until fork-tender, 12 to 15 minutes. Drain, transfer to a mixing bowl, and let cool.

Refill the pot with water and bring to a boil.

Meanwhile, mash the potatoes with a masher or a fork; some lumps are okay.

Add the 2 cups (250 g) flour, ½ cup (62 g) at a time, and knead until a stiff dough forms. Depending on the moisture content of your potatoes you may need a little more or less flour.

Form into 16 patties. Set aside.

In a skillet or frying pan, heat the oil and sauté the onion, mushrooms, and garlic until the mushrooms have reduced in volume by about half, 5 to 7 minutes.

Add the vegetable broth and tamari and bring to a simmer. Sprinkle in the remaining 2 tablespoons (16 g) flour and stir until thickened. Remove from the heat and stir in the peas.

Spoon the filling into the center of 8 of the patties. Place the remaining 8 patties on top and seal the edges securely by pressing them together.

Add about 4 sealed patties at a time to the boiling water and boil for 15 to 20 minutes, or until they float around freely. If they are still sinking to the bottom, they are not done yet.

YIELD: 8 BURGERS

Burger Oscar

87

Veal Oscar is a classic Swedish dish named after King Oscar II, who was partial to topping his meat with crab, asparagus, and béarnaise sauce. Of course we've veganized it here—to make it even better, of course—but it's still just as fancy pants, so make sure to set your table with nice white linens and get out your fanciest china.

FOR HOLLANDAISE THE WAY IT SHOULD TASTE SAUCE:

¼ cup (56 g) nondairy butter

2 tablespoons (16 g) all-purpose flour

1 cup (235 ml) plain soy creamer

1 tablespoon (15 ml) lemon juice

1 tablespoon (8 g) nutritional yeast

⅛ teaspoon cayenne pepper

Salt

FOR ASPARAGUS:

1 bunch asparagus

½ cup (120 ml) olive oil

¼ cup (60 ml) balsamic vinegar

Salt and pepper

FOR BURGERS:

1 recipe All-American Burger (page 82)

4 or 8 slices French or Italian bread, lightly toasted

DIRECTIONS:

To make the sauce: In a pot, melt the butter over high heat. Add the flour and whisk vigorously until smooth. Add the creamer, bring to a boil, and immediately remove from the heat. Stir in the lemon juice, nutritional yeast, cayenne, and salt to taste.

To make the asparagus: Snap each asparagus stalk at the natural break and discard the tough bottoms.

Add the asparagus, olive oil, vinegar, and salt and pepper to taste to a resealable bag and shake. Let sit for about 1 hour.

In a grill pan or on a barbecue, grill the asparagus until tender, 5 to 7 minutes, turning occasionally.

Place 1 burger on 1 slice of bread. Top with one-fourth of the asparagus and then pour on the sauce. Serve open-faced or top with another slice of bread. Repeat for the remaining 3 burgers.

Serve any remaining sauce in small bowls for dipping.

YIELD: 4 BURGERS

SERVING SUGGESTION

Serve with a nice plump baked potato, smothered in nondairy butter, nondairy sour cream (page 191), and chives.

Brisbane Burger from Down Under

88

Vegemite. Need I say more? Oh, and don't forget to grill these babies up on the bar-bee.

INGREDIENTS:

2 cups (288 g) vital wheat gluten flour

½ cup (60 g) whole wheat flour

½ cup (64 g) vegetable broth powder

1 tablespoon (6 g) freshly ground black pepper

1 cup (235 ml) water

¼ cup (68 g) ketchup

¼ cup (60 ml) vegetable oil

2 tablespoons (30 ml) soy sauce

1 tablespoon (15 ml) steak sauce

2 teaspoons (13 g) Vegemite

DIRECTIONS:

In a mixing bowl, combine the flours, vegetable broth powder, and pepper.

In a separate bowl, whisk together the water, ketchup, oil, soy sauce, steak sauce, and Vegemite.

Add the wet ingredients to the dry and knead together until well incorporated. Cover and let sit for about 20 minutes to rest.

Add the dry ingredients to the wet and knead to combine.

Form into 8 patties.

Barbecue over medium heat, 5 to 7 minutes per side, or bake at 350°F (180°C, or gas mark 4) on a baking sheet lined with parchment or a silicone baking mat, covered loosely with foil, for 15 minutes, then flip and bake for 15 minutes longer, until firm and warmed all the way through.

YIELD: 8 BURGERS

SERVING SUGGESTION

Serve this burger on toast with a thin layer of Vegemite spread evenly to add that salty, savory, tangy flavor the Aussies have come to know and love.

RECIPE NOTE

Can't find Vegemite? Try the British version, Marmite, but don't tell the Aussies that I told you to!

Earth Burger

These chunky, hearty, earthy burgers certainly qualify as hippie food. But, seriously, who doesn't love a hippie?

INGREDIENTS:

4 ounces (112 g) mushrooms, chopped

3 cloves garlic, minced

¼ cup (60 ml) olive oil, divided

2 cups (330 g) cooked wild rice blend

½ cup (75 g) corn kernels

1½ cups (107 g) chopped broccoli florets

1 cup (144 g) vital wheat gluten flour

½ cup (56 g) soy flour

½ cup (120 ml) water

Salt and pepper

DIRECTIONS:

Sauté the mushrooms and garlic in 2 tablespoons (30 ml) of the olive oil for 5 to 7 minutes, or until fragrant and translucent.

In a mixing bowl, combine the sautéed mushrooms and garlic, the remaining 2 tablespoons (30 ml) olive oil, rice, corn, broccoli, flours, water, and salt and pepper to taste. Refrigerate for at least 20 minutes to thicken a bit.

Preheat the oven to 375°F (190°C, or gas mark 5). Line a baking sheet with parchment or a silicone baking mat.

Form into 8 patties and place on the prepared baking sheet.

Bake for 25 minutes, uncovered, or until slightly firm and just beginning to brown.

YIELD: 8 BURGERS

SERVING SUGGESTION

Serve with sprouts, avocado, onions, tomatoes, or whatever your heart desires. Serve with a hearty garden salad topped with sunflower seeds and Creamy Balsamic Dressing (page 189) to really make it a hippie meal.

CHAPTER 9

BURGERS FOR THE HOLIDAYS

WHO SAYS YOU CAN'T HAVE A BURGER ON CHRISTMAS?

90 Fruity Holiday Brunch Burger

Lovingly referred to as oatmeal pie by my husband, this fruit-packed oatmeal burger makes a perfect brunch. I like to heat up a little extra fruit with a bit of agave to use as a topping. Some fruit combinations that work well are strawberries, blueberries, and raspberries; peaches and blueberries; or strawberries, bananas, and pineapple.

INGREDIENTS:

2 cups (160 g) dry oats

1 cup (120 g) whole wheat flour

1 cup (125 g) all-purpose flour

1 cup (220 g) firmly packed brown sugar

1 teaspoon baking powder

1 teaspoon baking soda

½ teaspoon ground cinnamon

¼ teaspoon ground nutmeg

¼ teaspoon ground cloves

¼ teaspoon salt

8 ounces (227 g) applesauce

¼ cup (60 ml) maple syrup

¼ cup (56 g) nondairy butter, melted

1 teaspoon pure vanilla extract

1½ cups (225 to 250 g) chopped fruit of choice (if using frozen fruit, thaw before using), tossed with a bit of sugar (optional)

DIRECTIONS:

Preheat the oven to 350°F (180°C, or gas mark 4). Line a baking sheet with parchment or a silicone baking mat.

In a mixing bowl, combine the oats, flours, brown sugar, baking powder, baking soda, cinnamon, nutmeg, cloves, and salt.

In a separate bowl, combine the applesauce, maple syrup, butter, and vanilla.

Add the dry ingredients to the wet and mix well, using your hands, until a nice dough forms.

Divide the dough into 12 equal pieces. Form into patties.

Place 6 patties on the prepared baking sheet. Add about ¼ cup (38 to 41 g) fruit to the center of each patty. Top with the remaining 6 patties and seal the edges by pinching them together.

Bake for 20 to 25 minutes, or until golden. Let cool slightly, because the filling will be hot.

YIELD: 6 BURGERS

SERVING SUGGESTION

Top this with extra fruit, some vanilla nondairy yogurt, and a sprig o' mint.

91 Savory Noodle Kugel Burger

Let me start off by saying that I am not Jewish, and I make no claims to the authenticity or kosherness of this kugel burger. I know that this is certainly not acceptable for Passover, but it might be okay for Chanukah. What I will stand by, however, is the cheesy goodness of, what is to me, mac and cheeze on a bun. Warning: This is not low fat, this is not low cal, this is not health food in any sense of the word. What it is? Pure rich and delicious decadence.

INGREDIENTS:

8 ounces (227 g) uncooked macaroni

2 cups (220 g) shredded potatoes

12 ounces (340 g) extra-firm tofu, drained, pressed, and crumbled to resemble ricotta

¼ cup (60 g) nondairy cream cheese

¼ cup (56 g) nondairy butter

¼ cup (30 g) nutritional yeast

¼ cup (65 g) raw cashews, ground into a fine powder

1 tablespoon (8 g) onion powder

1 tablespoon (8 g) garlic powder

1 tablespoon (18 g) white miso

Pinch of paprika

Salt and pepper

1 cup (115 g) crushed cornflakes or bread crumbs

Oil, for frying (optional)

DIRECTIONS:

Cook the macaroni in salted water according to the package instructions.

While the macaroni is cooking, in a large mixing bowl, combine the potatoes, tofu, cream cheese, butter, yeast, cashew powder, onion powder, garlic powder, miso, paprika, and salt and pepper to taste. Using your hands, mash everything together until well combined and uniform.

Add the drained, cooked macaroni noodles, and mash again until well incorporated. Finally, mash in the cornflakes.

Form into 8 patties. Cook as desired.

Panfry in plenty of oil over medium heat for 5 minutes per side, or until golden and crispy, or bake at 350°F (180°C, or gas mark 4), uncovered, on a baking sheet lined with parchment or a silicone baking mat, for about 15 minutes, then flip and bake for 15 minutes longer, until firm and just beginning to brown.

YIELD: 8 BURGERS

SERVING SUGGESTION

Serve on a soft white bun, an onion bun, or a potato roll, schmeared with vegan mayo (page 191). To help balance out this fat-laden meal, serve up a nice side of broccoli, asparagus, or peas.

RECIPE NOTE

Not in the mood for burgers? Pack this mixture into a square baking dish and serve it as a casserole. Just bake it, uncovered, at 350°F (180°C, or gas mark 4) for 15 to 20 minutes, or until the top is golden and crispy.

Matzo Burger

92

As I said before, I'm not Jewish. But I am fascinated with kosher dietary law. Working in the food service industry has taught me a lot about what can be eaten for Passover and how certain ingredients that are considered kosher the rest of the year are not necessarily kosher for Passover. That being said, I feel pretty confident that if you buy kosher-for-Passover ingredients to make this burger—if, of course, you eat soy during Passover—then it most certainly can find a seat at the Seder table. After all, it's almost like a latke . . . but with a bit of sass.

INGREDIENTS:

2 tablespoons (28 g) nondairy butter

2 cups (320 g) finely diced yellow onion

1 tablespoon (15 g) minced garlic

2 pounds (908 g) peeled and shredded russet potatoes, rinsed and drained in cold water

2 cups (240 g) matzo meal

1 cup (240 g) nondairy sour cream, store-bought or homemade (page 191)

½ cup (120 ml) soy or other nondairy milk

1 teaspoon paprika

½ teaspoon salt

½ teaspoon black pepper

Oil, for frying

DIRECTIONS:

In a frying pan or cast-iron skillet, melt the butter over high heat.

Add the onion and garlic and sauté for about 5 minutes, or until fragrant, translucent, and just beginning to brown. Set aside.

In a mixing bowl, combine the potatoes, matzo meal, sour cream, milk, paprika, salt, and pepper. Add the onion and garlic mixture and knead to combine.

Form into 8 patties. Line a plate with paper towels.

Preheat ¼ inch (6 mm) oil in a frying pan over medium-high heat. The oil is ready when a piece of dough dropped into it sizzles immediately. Add 2 or 3 patties at a time to the hot oil and fry for 3 to 5 minutes per side, or until golden and crispy. Transfer to the plate to absorb any excess oil, and repeat to fry the remaining 5 or 6 patties in 2 more batches.

YIELD: 8 BURGERS

SERVING SUGGESTION

I prefer this served traditionally with a dollop of nondairy sour cream or applesauce.

Oktoberfest Kraut Burger

SOY FREE

93

No vegan beer garden in your town? No biggie. Make your own kraut burgers to snack on between those pints of brew. Speaking of kraut, choose yours wisely. True sauerkraut is fermented, not pickled in vinegar. Check ingredient labels and choose one that only contains cabbage, salt, and spices.

INGREDIENTS:

2 cups (288 g) vital wheat gluten flour

¼ cup (30 g) nutritional yeast

1 tablespoon (8 g) garlic powder

1 tablespoon (8 g) onion powder

1 tablespoon (2 g) dried parsley

1 teaspoon freshly ground black pepper

1½ cups (355 ml) vegetable broth

½ cup (120 g) sauerkraut, drained

SERVING SUGGESTION

Serve up with lots of extra kraut, grilled onions, and spicy brown mustard on a soft white bun. Making a full-on meal? Add sides of roasted brussels sprouts and Smoky Potato Salad (page 214, and pictured here) to your plate.

DIRECTIONS:

Preheat the oven to 350°F (180°C, or gas mark 4). Line a baking sheet with parchment or a silicone baking mat.

In a mixing bowl, combine the flour, nutritional yeast, garlic powder, onion powder, parsley, and black pepper. Slowly add the vegetable broth and stir to combine.

Add the sauerkraut and knead until uniform and consistent. Cover and let sit for about 20 minutes to allow the gluten to rest.

Form into 8 patties and place on the prepared baking sheet. Cover the entire pan loosely with foil.

Bake for 20 minutes, then flip and bake for 20 minutes longer, until firm and warmed all the way through.

YIELD: 8 BURGERS

94 Cinco de Mayo Burger

Feliz Cinco de Mayo! For most of us who celebrate this holiday, it's all about getting your drink on, so who wants to be strapped down in the kitchen with hugely elaborate recipes? This one is so easy, and quick, that you'll be able to get back to the party in minutes!

INGREDIENTS:

12 ounces (340 g) soy chorizo

1 can (15 ounces, or 420 g) frijoles negro (black beans), drained

1 cup (125 g) all-purpose flour

½ cup (50 g) chopped scallion

½ cup (8 g) finely chopped fresh cilantro

Oil or nonstick spray, for frying

DIRECTIONS:

In a skillet, panfry soy chorizo and beans until they are completely warmed through and hot, 5 to 7 minutes.

Remove from the heat and stir in the flour. Let cool.

Using your hands, knead in the scallion and cilantro until you get a soft, smooth mixture.

Form into 5 patties and panfry in a smidge of oil over medium heat until a nice crispy crust forms, about 3 to 5 minutes per side. Now go get your tequila on!

YIELD: 5 BURGERS (OF COURSE!)

SERVING SUGGESTION

Serve with tortilla chips and salsa or guacamole, or with Spanish rice and beans. To garnish, think burrito fillings: avocado, nondairy sour cream, salsa, peppers, onions . . .

RECIPE NOTE

Looking for a drink to serve at your fiesta? Don't rely on artificially flavored, artificially colored, sickeningly sweet pre-made margarita mixes. Making a real margarita is simple: Add 4 ounces (118 ml) tequila, 3 ounces (89 ml) fresh lime juice, 1 ounce (20 ml) simple syrup, and 3 ounces (89 ml) triple sec to a shaker filled with ice cubes. Shake and pour into a salt-rimmed glass with a wedge of lime.

All-the-Fixins' Holiday Burger

This here burger was the brainchild of my bestie, Jen. She said if I could pack an entire holiday dinner into a burger, she would be in heaven. So, I gave it a shot. I invited her over and had her test it out. She said it was like crack and . . . there you have it.

INGREDIENTS:

1 tablespoon (14 g) nondairy butter

1 cup (160 g) diced onion

2 tablespoons (30 g) minced garlic

4 cups (900 g) cooked mashed potatoes

4 cups (800 g) prepared bread stuffing (see note)

1 can (14 ounces, or 392 g) cut green beans, drained

1 cup (96 g) French's French Fried Onions

Salt and pepper

Oil, for frying (optional)

DIRECTIONS:

In a skillet over medium-high heat, melt the butter, add the onion and garlic, and sauté until just beginning to brown, 3 to 5 minutes.

Transfer to a bowl, add the potatoes, stuffing, green beans, fried onions, and salt and pepper to taste. Knead to combine.

Form into 8 patties. Cook as desired.

Panfry in oil for 3 to 5 minutes per side, or until crispy and golden, or bake at 350°F (180°C, or gas mark 4), on a baking sheet lined with parchment or a silicone baking mat, for about 20 minutes, flipping halfway through. Everything is already cooked—you just need to heat them up!

YIELD: 8 BURGERS

RECIPE NOTE

I use boxed stuffing, but any bread-based stuffing will work fine. In fact, a few slices of stale bread, cut into cubes and mixed with butter and vegetable broth, then baked, makes a pretty darn good stuffing!

SERVING SUGGESTION

Make this burger as an alternative to a huge elaborate holiday dinner or make it the day after out of the leftovers from the big meal.

96 Green Bean Almondine Burger

This burger helped my partner in vegan crime, Celine, fall back in love with mushrooms. Serve it as a non-traditional, traditional side at any holiday party you head to, and I guarantee the guests will rejoice.

FOR ALMONDINE:

3 cups (705 ml) water

1 pound (454 g) fresh green beans, ends trimmed

2 tablespoons (28 g) nondairy butter

8 ounces (227 g) mushrooms, sliced

1 cup (160 g) diced onion

2 tablespoons (30 g) minced garlic

Salt and pepper

¼ cup (27 g) slivered or sliced almonds

¼ cup (25 g) imitation bacon bits, store-bought or homemade (optional, page 185)

FOR BURGERS:

1 recipe Almondine, divided

¼ cup (64 g) almond butter

½ cup (62 g) all-purpose flour

½ cup (72 g) vital wheat gluten flour

Salt and pepper

Oil, for frying (optional)

SERVING SUGGESTION

Serve on a toasted piece of French bread or with a schmear of vegan mayo and topped with extra almondine.

DIRECTIONS:

To make the almondine: In your largest frying pan, add the water and bring to a boil (you can add a pinch of salt to the water if you choose).

Add the beans and boil for 3 minutes. Remove from the heat, drain, and set aside.

Dry the pan and add the butter. Melt the butter over high heat. Add the mushrooms, onion, and garlic. Sauté until the mushrooms have reduced in size by half, about 7 minutes. Season with salt and pepper.

Add the almonds and bacon bits. Cook for 2 minutes longer.

Add the green beans. Toss to coat, and cook for 3 to 5 minutes longer.

To make the burgers: Divide the Almondine recipe in half. Set half aside.

Place half the Almondine in the food processor along with the almond butter, flours, and salt and pepper to taste. Pulse until crumbly.

Form into 4 patties and cook as desired.

To bake, place on a baking sheet lined with parchment or a silicone mat, cover with foil, and bake at 350°F (180°C, or gas mark 4) for 15 minutes, then flip and bake 15 minutes longer. Or panfry in oil for 3 to 5 minutes per side until a golden crust forms.

Top with the reserved almondine.

YIELD: 4 BURGERS

CHAPTER 10

LOOSE "MEAT" SANDWICHES

OOEY, GOOEY, CRUMBLY STUFF THAT FITS NICELY BETWEEN TWO PIECES OF BREAD!

Deli-Style No-Tuna Melt

WHEAT FREE

97

This tastes like tuna salad. Really! Use this recipe as a guideline, but feel free to add or take out any ingredients you feel should be in your "tuna" melt.

INGREDIENTS:

8 ounces (227 g) plain soy tempeh,* crumbled into tiny pieces

¼ cup (60 g) sweet pickle relish

½ cup (112 g) vegan mayonnaise, store-bought or homemade (page 191)

½ cup (80 g) diced red onion

¼ teaspoon dill

Salt and pepper

DIRECTIONS:

Mix together all the ingredients in a bowl. Refrigerate until ready to use. You can use this on a sandwich or on a bed of greens for a no-tuna salad.

If making a melt, preheat a cast-iron skillet or pan over high heat.

To get the best browning without added fat and calories, spray the pan with nonstick spray, then cook until browned, applying pressure from the top with a spatula, then spray the top with cooking spray, flip, and apply pressure until browned.

YIELD: ENOUGH FOR 4 TO 6 SANDWICHES

RECIPE NOTE

Some people find that steaming the tempeh prior to crumbling it mellows the flavor a bit. If you are the type that is tempeh hesitant or just plain old don't like tempeh, don't give up on this salad. Cut the tempeh block in half and steam in or over simmering water for 20 minutes. Some folks even say that this helps make the tempeh more digestible.

SERVING SUGGESTION

This is perfect grilled between 2 slices of sourdough, with Dijon mustard, 2 slices of Roma tomato, and a slice of nondairy cheese, as shown here.

98 Tofu Egg Salad Sammy

I used to love the egg salad sandwiches my mom made for us. They were pretty plain. No onions, no pickles, no capers. Just eggs, mayo, and a smidge of mustard. Well, I'm all grown up now, with grown-up taste buds. This is my take on my childhood favorite. If you are worried about the fat, you can reduce the amount of oil in the pan, or eliminate it altogether and use an olive oil cooking spray instead. For the mayo, Trader Joe's sell a way less fattening vegan mayo, or you could use plain soy yogurt instead, but it will be tangier. I didn't make this as a low-fat recipe, because, made as written, it tastes soooo good! As always, try to use organic ingredients when possible. If you want an even more flavorful version, sauté some mushrooms along with the onions and garlic.

INGREDIENTS:

2 tablespoons (30 ml) olive oil

1 cup (160 g) diced white or yellow onion

4 cloves garlic, minced

12 ounces (340 g) extra-firm tofu, drained, pressed, and cubed

¼ cup (30 g) nutritional yeast

¼ teaspoon turmeric

½ teaspoon ground mustard

⅛ teaspoon dill

⅛ teaspoon paprika

½ cup (112 g) vegan mayonnaise, store-bought or homemade (page 191)

1 tablespoon (15 g) yellow mustard

½ teaspoon black salt (optional)

Pepper

DIRECTIONS:

In a skillet, heat the oil over medium-high heat and sauté the onion and garlic until fragrant, 3 to 4 minutes.

Add the tofu and sauté for 10 to 12 minutes, or until golden.

Lower the heat and add the nutritional yeast, turmeric, ground mustard, dill, and paprika.

Fold until well coated, then remove from the heat and let cool.

Add the mayonnaise and mustard. Mix well.

Add the salt and pepper to taste.

Keep refrigerated until ready to serve.

YIELD: ENOUGH FOR 8 WRAPS OR SANDWICHES

RECIPE NOTE

I like to cut my tofu into tiny cubes for this recipe, because I like the toothier feel to the cubes. Crumble it to make it more "yolky." Cube it to make it more "eggy."

SERVING SUGGESTION

Serve on sprouted grain bread, in a whole grain tortilla, or on a bed of greens. And enjoy outside, picnic-style, if you can!

Chicken Salad Sammy

WHEAT FREE

Although there is a lot of tofu in this salad, the real star is the crunch from all the fresh, raw veggies.

INGREDIENTS:

12 ounces (340 g) extra-firm tofu, drained and pressed

2 tablespoons (30 ml) olive oil

4 to 6 cloves garlic, minced

½ cup (54 g) shredded carrot

1 red onion, chopped

2 stalks celery, chopped

½ cup (60 g) walnut pieces

1 cup (150 g) grapes (green or red, or even raisins), halved

1 cup (224 g) vegan mayonnaise, store-bought or homemade (page 191)

Salt and pepper

DIRECTIONS:

Chop up the tofu into tiny, tiny, tiny pieces.

Heat the olive oil in a skillet over medium-high heat and add the garlic. Sauté for a minute.

Add the tofu and sauté until golden, 7 to 10 minutes.

Remove from the heat and let cool.

Add carrot, onion, celery, walnuts, grapes, mayonnaise, and salt and pepper to taste. Stir to combine.

Chill before serving.

YIELD: ENOUGH FOR 4 TO 6 SANDWICHES

SERVING SUGGESTION

Serve on a sandwich, in a wrap, or on a bed of greens, or eat it with a fork right out of the bowl!

RECIPE NOTE

A tip for pressing tofu: After you've drained the excess liquid from the package, place the block sandwiched between two folded dish towels. Place a heavy book or pan on top to gently press the moisture out and let sit for 30 minutes to one hour to completely press.

100 Pulled Pork Sammy

SOY FREE

These sammies are great to serve in the summertime, or when you have people over for a casual gathering.

FOR SEITAN:

1½ cups (216 g) vital wheat gluten flour

½ cup (60 g) whole wheat flour

¼ cup (30 g) nutritional yeast

1 yellow onion, finely diced

½ cup (120 ml) water

¼ cup (60 ml) steak sauce

2 tablespoons (33 g) tomato paste

1 tablespoon (15 g) Dijon mustard

FOR BROTH:

2 cups (470 ml) vegetable broth

½ cup (110 g) firmly packed brown sugar

2 tablespoons (14 g) paprika

2 tablespoons (16 g) onion powder

2 tablespoons (16 g) garlic powder

1 tablespoon (7 g) black pepper

1 teaspoon cayenne pepper

1 teaspoon liquid smoke

1 teaspoon ground cumin

DIRECTIONS:

To make the seitan: In a mixing bowl, combine the flours and nutritional yeast.

In a separate bowl, combine the onion, water, steak sauce, tomato paste, and mustard.

Add the wet ingredients to the dry and knead until well combined. Let sit for 20 minutes.

To make the broth: Combine all the broth ingredients in a stockpot and bring to a boil.

Divide the seitan dough into 4 pieces and carefully drop into the boiling broth.

Lower the heat to a simmer, cover, and simmer for about 30 minutes, or until most of the moisture is absorbed, stirring often so the seitan does not stick to the bottom of the pot. Remove from the heat.

Using a fork, pull apart the "pork" seitan and pile onto sandwiches.

YIELD: ENOUGH FOR 4 TO 6 SANDWICHES

SERVING SUGGESTION

Serve Po' Boy style on a French roll topped with a mountain of Creamy BBQ Coleslaw (page 215).

Philly Cheese Steak

Serve this classic sandwich on game night to satisfy those manly cravings.

FOR CHEEZY SAUCE:

2 cups (470 ml) soy creamer

½ cup (60 g) nutritional yeast

½ cup (65 g) raw cashews

1 tablespoon (16 g) tahini

2 tablespoons (36 g) white miso

2 tablespoons (16 g) cornstarch

1 tablespoon (8 g) onion powder

1 tablespoon (8 g) garlic powder

1 tablespoon (8 g) ground mustard

FOR SANDWICHES:

Vegetable oil, for frying

2 large white onions, sliced or diced

2 red, green, or yellow bell peppers, sliced into thin strips or diced

½ recipe Green Castle Sliders (page 87), prepared but not sliced

Salt and pepper

4 French rolls

DIRECTIONS:

To make the cheezy sauce: Place all the ingredients in a blender or food processor and process until smooth. Place in a saucepan. Heat over low heat until it thickens, constantly stirring so it doesn't get clumpy or scorch.

To make the sandwiches: Slice the slider dough into strips about 1 inch (2.5 cm) wide and 4 to 6 inches (10 to 15 cm) long.

In a large frying pan, preheat about 3 tablespoons (45 ml) of oil, adding more later as you continue cooking. Sauté some of the onions, some of the peppers, and some of the slider strips, in amounts you like for your sammies. Season with salt and pepper. Pile high onto the French rolls and drizzle with the cheezy sauce.

YIELD: 2½ CUPS (588 ML) CHEEZY SAUCE AND ENOUGH FILLING TO MAKE 4 SANDWICHES

SERVING SUGGESTION

Serve with Papa's Spicy Mac Salad (page 210) or a side of fries using any extra cheese sauce for dipping.

CHAPTER 11

CONDIMENTS AND SAUCES

TOPPINGS, SAUCES, DIPS, AND SUCH TO GIVE YOUR BURGERS THAT PERFECT TOUCH

- Nacho Cheesy Sauce
- Tangy Tahini Sauce
- Quick and Simple BBQ Sauce
- Indian-Spiced Mayo
- Chipotle Dipping Sauce
- Taco Seasoning
- Imitation Bacon Bits

- Mom's Mango Salsa
- Simple Pesto
- Sun-Dried Tomato Aioli
- Garlic Artichoke Spread
- Chunky Marinara
- Aioli Dipping Sauce
- Creamy Balsamic Dressing

- Vegan Mayonnaise
- Nondairy Sour Cream
- Sweet Mustard Sauce
- Pineapple Orange Pomegranate Relish
- Tzatziki Sauce
- Thai Peanut Sauce

Nacho Cheesy Sauce

Perfect to top the Jalapeño Cornbread Burger (page 125) but also great on tortilla chips, tacos, burritos, and even chili.

INGREDIENTS:

2 cups (470 ml) soy creamer

½ cup (60 g) nutritional yeast

½ cup (65 g) raw cashews

1 tablespoon (16 g) tahini

2 tablespoons (36 g) white miso

2 tablespoons (16 g) cornstarch

1 tablespoon (8 g) onion powder

1 tablespoon (8 g) garlic powder

1 tablespoon (8 g) ground mustard

1 teaspoon ground cumin

1 teaspoon hot sauce, or more to taste

2 to 4 slices jarred or canned jalapeños

1 tablespoon (15 ml) juice from jar of jalapeños

DIRECTIONS:

Place all the ingredients in a blender or food processor and process until smooth.

Place in a saucepan. Heat over low heat until it thickens, stirring constantly so it doesn't get clumpy or scorch. Store in an airtight container in the refrigerator until ready to use.

YIELD: 2½ CUPS (590 G)

Tangy Tahini Sauce

This tangy sauce works so well as a spread for many of the burgers in this book, including the Super Quinoa Burger (page 95) and The Trifecta Burger (page 111). It is also delicious as a salad dressing or dip for veggies.

INGREDIENTS:

1 container (6 ounces, or 170 g) plain soy yogurt

3 tablespoons (48 g) tahini

2 tablespoons (30 ml) sesame oil

1 tablespoon (15 ml) lemon juice

½ teaspoon dill

½ teaspoon paprika

Salt and pepper

DIRECTIONS:

Place all the ingredients in a blender and blend until smooth, or whisk together very well.

Store in an airtight container in the refrigerator until ready to use.

YIELD: 1 CUP (240 G)

Quick and Simple BBQ Sauce

It takes longer to drive to the store and buy a bottle than it does to simmer up your own sweet and sassy barbecue sauce!

INGREDIENTS:

1 tablespoon (15 ml) olive oil

1 yellow onion, finely diced

16 ounces (454 g) tomato sauce

1 teaspoon onion powder

1 teaspoon garlic powder

2 tablespoons (30 ml) apple cider vinegar

2 tablespoons (44 g) molasses

½ teaspoon freshly ground black pepper

2 tablespoons (40 g) grape jelly

2 tablespoons (30 ml) soy sauce

¼ teaspoon liquid smoke (optional)

DIRECTIONS:

Heat the oil in a skillet and sauté the onion until fragrant and translucent, 5 to 7 minutes.

Add the tomato sauce, onion powder, garlic powder, vinegar, molasses, pepper, jelly, and soy sauce and bring to a simmer. Simmer over low heat, uncovered, for about 10 minutes, stirring occasionally. Remove from the heat. Stir in the liquid smoke.

If you don't like chunks of onion in your barbecue sauce, let cool and run through a blender or food processor until smooth.

Use as you would any barbecue sauce.

YIELD: 3 CUPS (750 G)

Indian-Spiced Mayo

Here's another aioli-type spread that tastes great on the Middle Eastern burgers in chapter 4.

INGREDIENTS:

1 cup (225 g) vegan mayonnaise, store-bought or homemade (page 191)

1 tablespoon (8 g) garam masala

Pinch of paprika

Pinch of turmeric

Salt and pepper

DIRECTIONS:

Combine all the ingredients in an airtight container and keep refrigerated until ready to use.

YIELD: 1 CUP (225 G)

Chipotle Dipping Sauce

I especially like the way the spiciness of this sauce plays off the sweetness of the Chipotle Sweet Potato Burger (page 126) and Sweet Potato Fries (page 206). This sauce also works well as a spread for sandwiches, or even on the bun under your Edamame Burger (page 46).

INGREDIENTS:

1 cup (240 g) nondairy sour cream, store-bought or homemade (page 191)

½ teaspoon chipotle powder

½ teaspoon garlic powder

¼ teaspoon dillweed

Salt and pepper

DIRECTIONS:

Place all the ingredients in a bowl and mix well.

Keep refrigerated until ready to use. The longer you refrigerate it, the more the chipotle flavor will develop.

YIELD: 1 CUP (240 G)

Taco Seasoning

When I buy it, I usually buy the Taco Bell brand because it doesn't have any whey. If you don't have, or can't find, a vegan one, you can make your own by mixing together the following ingredients and storing it in an airtight container.

INGREDIENTS:

1 tablespoon (8 g) garlic powder

1 tablespoon (8 g) onion powder

1 tablespoon (13 g) sugar

1 tablespoon (7 g) ground cumin

1 tablespoon (7 g) paprika

2 tablespoons (16 g) chili powder

1½ teaspoons salt

DIRECTIONS:

Place all the ingredients in a small airtight container and shake vigorously.

Two tablespoons (16 g) of this mix roughly equals one packet of store-bought taco seasoning.

YIELD: ½ CUP (128 G)

imitation Bacon Bits

I love a challenge, so when asked about the hydrogenated fats in imitation bacon bits, I started on a quest. I normally don't buy premade meat analogs anyway, so why not figure out how to make these little bits of bacon-y goodness on my own? Of course, buying a jar of Bac-Os is still the easiest. But, if you are a smidge adventurous, try this.

INGREDIENTS:

2 tablespoons (30 ml) liquid smoke

1 scant cup (225 ml) water

1 cup (96 g) TVP granules

¼ teaspoon salt

A few drops vegan red food coloring (optional)

3 tablespoons (45 ml) canola or other vegetable oil

DIRECTIONS:

To a measuring cup, add the liquid smoke, then fill with the water to get 1 cup (235 ml).

In a microwave-safe dish, combine the liquid smoke mixture, TVP granules, salt, and red food coloring. Cover tightly with plastic wrap and microwave for 5 to 6 minutes. Alternatively, bring the water to a boil, pour over the TVP granules mixed with the salt, mix in the liquid smoke and red food coloring, cover, and let sit for 10 minutes.

Preheat a frying pan with the oil.

Add the reconstituted TVP to the pan and toss to make sure it all gets coated with oil.

Panfry until desired crispness. Stir often. You don't necessarily want to brown them, but rather dry them out, about 10 minutes.

Allow to cool completely before transferring to an air-tight container. Store in the refrigerator. Should last at least a week, but probably much longer.

YIELD: ABOUT 1 CUP (100 G)

Mom's Mango Salsa

My mom rocks. She always makes sure that there is enough for me to eat when I visit. This is her famous mango salsa. I could live on this stuff alone while I'm at her house.

INGREDIENTS:

1 mango, peeled, seeded, and diced

½ cup (8 g) finely chopped fresh cilantro

½ cup (80 g) finely diced red onion

1 teaspoon garlic powder

½ teaspoon salt, or more to taste

½ teaspoon black pepper

1 serrano chile, seeded, cored, and finely diced

DIRECTIONS:

In a bowl, combine all the ingredients and refrigerate overnight to enhance the flavor.

Serve with tortilla chips, or pile on top of some of the spicier burgers for a nice contrast in flavor and texture.

YIELD: ABOUT 1½ CUPS (375 G)

Simple Pesto

I usually double this recipe, using half for the Sun-Dried Tomato and Pesto Burger (page 68) or Garlic, Mushroom, and Onion Seitanic Stuffer (page 105) and reserving the other half to spread on a toasted bun or throw on some pasta later.

INGREDIENTS:

14 large fresh basil leaves

2 or 3 cloves garlic

½ teaspoon coarse sea salt

1 tablespoon (8 g) toasted pine nuts

1 tablespoon (8 g) raw walnut pieces

1 tablespoon (8 g) nutritional yeast

3 tablespoons (45 ml) olive oil

DIRECTIONS:

In a food processor, combine the basil, garlic, salt, pine nuts, walnuts, and nutritional yeast and process until a purée is formed.

Drizzle in the oil and pulse a few more times to combine.

YIELD: ½ CUP (130 G)

Sun-Dried Tomato Aioli

This works well on almost any of the burgers in this book, and as a sandwich or bagel spread.

INGREDIENTS:

2 cloves garlic

¼ cup (28 g) sun-dried tomatoes packed in oil

¼ teaspoon paprika

¼ cup (30 g) pine nuts

¾ cup (168 g) vegan mayonnaise, store-bought or homemade (page 191)

Salt and pepper

DIRECTIONS:

In a food processor, combine the garlic, tomatoes, and paprika and process until smooth. Transfer to a bowl.

Add the pine nuts, mayonnaise, and salt and pepper to taste. Stir to combine.

Store in an airtight container, in the fridge, until ready to use.

YIELD: JUST OVER 1 CUP (250 G)

Garlic Artichoke Spread

This works well as a burger or sandwich spread and as a dip for crackers and veggies. It is especially yummy on the Baba Ghanoush Burger (page 53).

INGREDIENTS:

2 tablespoons (30 ml) plus ¼ cup (60 ml) olive oil, divided

1 yellow onion, chopped

2 tablespoons (30 g) minced garlic

½ teaspoon ground cumin

Pinch of salt and freshly cracked pepper

1 can (14 ounces, or 392 g) artichoke hearts, drained and roughly chopped

½ cup (60 g) pine nuts (optional)

DIRECTIONS:

Preheat the 2 tablespoons (30 ml) oil over medium-high heat in a flat-bottomed skillet.

Add the onion, garlic, cumin, salt, and pepper. Sauté until translucent and fragrant and the edges of the onions just start to turn brown, 5 to 7 minutes.

Transfer to a blender or food processor (I prefer a blender for this), add the artichoke hearts and remaining ¼ cup (60 ml) oil, and blend until smooth.

Transfer to a bowl and mix in the pine nuts.

YIELD: JUST UNDER 3 CUPS (685 G)

Chunky Marinara

This sauce is great for dipping Fried Zucchini (page 207), on pasta, and in the Zucchini Mushroom Burgers (page 70).

INGREDIENTS:

28 ounces (795 g) diced tomatoes with juice, no salt added

8 ounces (227 g) tomato sauce

6 ounces (170 g) tomato paste

1 tablespoon (2 g) dried basil

1 tablespoon (12 g) sugar

1 tablespoon (22 g) molasses

2 tablespoons (30 ml) olive oil

6 cloves garlic, minced

1 yellow onion, finely diced

DIRECTIONS:

Place the tomatoes, sauce, paste, basil, sugar, and molasses in a large stockpot. Bring to a simmer over medium-low heat.

Meanwhile, in a skillet, heat the olive oil and sauté the garlic and onion and until the garlic is fragrant and the onion is translucent, about 10 minutes.

Add the garlic and onion to the pot. Cover and continue to simmer for 20 minutes.

Uncover and simmer for 10 minutes.

YIELD: JUST UNDER 4 CUPS (980 G), OR ENOUGH FOR 2 POUNDS (905 G) PASTA

Aioli Dipping Sauce

This basic aioli can be your inspiration to never again be tempted to use plain old mayo—unless, of course, you love plain old mayo (like I do!).

INGREDIENTS:

⅔ cup (150 g) vegan mayonnaise, store-bought or homemade (page 191)

⅓ cup (80 g) nondairy sour cream, store-bought or homemade (page 191)

2 tablespoons (30 ml) extra-virgin olive oil

1½ tablespoons (23 ml) fresh lemon juice

3 tablespoons (9 g) chopped fresh basil

2 tablespoons (12 g) chopped fresh chives

1 tablespoon (15 g) minced garlic

1 tablespoon (8 g) lemon zest

½ teaspoon sea salt

½ teaspoon freshly cracked pepper

DIRECTIONS:

In small bowl, stir together the mayonnaise, sour cream, olive oil, and lemon juice.

Stir in the basil, chives, garlic, lemon zest, salt, and pepper.

Cover and refrigerate for at least 30 minutes, or until ready to use.

YIELD: 1½ CUPS (338 G)

Creamy Balsamic Dressing

This dressing (featured on the Scarborough Fair Tofu Burger on page 84) is my answer to a creamy garlic dressing that is served at one of my favorite Italian restaurants. Unfortunately for me, that dressing contains beef consommé and, therefore, is not vegan.

INGREDIENTS:

12 ounces (340 g) extra-firm tofu, drained but not pressed

½ cup (120 ml) olive oil

¼ cup (60 ml) balsamic vinegar

1 tablespoon (8 g) garlic powder

1 tablespoon (8 g) onion powder

Salt and pepper

DIRECTIONS:

Place all the ingredients in a blender and process until smooth.

Keep refrigerated in an airtight container until ready to use. Lasts about 1 week.

YIELD: 1½ CUPS (375 G)

Vegan Mayonnaise

No need to worry if your local market doesn't carry egg-free mayo. Just whip up some of your own. This recipe works very well as a sandwich spread (pictured here and on page 167) or in any of the mayonnaise-based dressings right here in this book. As long as you use wheat-free vinegar, this mayo is indeed wheat-free.

INGREDIENTS:

7 ounces (195 g) extra-firm tofu, drained and pressed

¼ cup (35 g) raw cashews, ground into a very fine powder

1 tablespoon (15 ml) lemon juice

1 tablespoon (12 g) raw sugar or (21 g) agave nectar

1½ teaspoons brown or Dijon mustard

1 teaspoon apple cider or rice wine vinegar

½ teaspoon sea salt

6 tablespoons (90 ml) canola oil

DIRECTIONS:

Place the tofu, cashews, lemon juice, sugar, mustard, vinegar, and salt in a blender or food processor and process until smooth.

Slowly drizzle in the oil and pulse until you get the consistency that you like.

Store in an airtight container in the refrigerator for up to 2 weeks.

YIELD: ALMOST 2 CUPS (450 G)

Nondairy Sour Cream

Although nondairy versions of traditionally dairy products are becoming more readily available, you might occasionally need to whip up a delicious batch of your own, especially if you are making the Three Bean Chili Burgers on page 137 or the Denver Omelet Burger on page 21 (where this recipe is pictured).

INGREDIENTS:

7 ounces (195 g) extra-firm tofu, drained well and pressed

¼ cup (28 g) raw cashews, ground into a fine powder

1 tablespoon (15 ml) white rice vinegar

1 tablespoon (15 ml) lemon or lime juice

1 tablespoon (18 g) white miso

1 tablespoon (15 ml) canola oil

DIRECTIONS:

Place all the ingredients in a blender or food processor and process until very, very smooth and creamy. Keep refrigerated in an airtight container until ready to use. Should last up to 1 week.

YIELD: ABOUT 1½ CUPS (345 G)

Sweet Mustard Sauce

This innocent sauce offers a bit of sweet relief when slathered onto some of the more spicy burgers in this book. It is especially tasty on the Jalapeño Cheddar Burger (page 135).

INGREDIENTS:

½ cup (120 g) vegan mayonnaise, store-bought or homemade (page 191)

2 tablespoons (42 g) agave nectar

2 tablespoons (30 g) Dijon mustard

1 tablespoon (6 g) finely diced chives

Salt and pepper

DIRECTIONS:

Whisk together all the ingredients.

Store in an airtight container in the refrigerator until ready to use.

YIELD: ¾ CUP (190 G)

Pineapple Orange Pomegranate Relish

This relish adds a tropical touch to anything you top with it and is an essential component to the Jamaican Jerk Burger on page 140.

INGREDIENTS:

1 cup (235 ml) pineapple juice

½ cup (120 ml) orange juice

¼ cup (60 ml) olive oil

1 cup (181 g) crushed pineapple

1 cup (135 g) pomegranate seeds

½ cup (50 g) finely chopped scallion

Salt and pepper

DIRECTIONS:

In a stockpot, bring the pineapple juice, orange juice, olive oil, and crushed pineapple to a boil. Lower the heat to a simmer and simmer for 20 minutes.

Remove from heat and stir in the pomegranate seeds, scallion, and salt and pepper to taste.

Refrigerate until ready to use.

YIELD: 3 CUPS (735 G)

Tzatziki Sauce

Fresh and tangy, this sauce works well with falafel, in a pita sandwich, or as a dip for warm pita triangles or flatbread. It is also great on Lizzy's Lentil Daal Burger on page 57.

INGREDIENTS:

12 ounces (340 g) plain soy or other nondairy yogurt

1½ cups (200 g) seeded and finely diced cucumber

1 tablespoon (3 g) fresh dill

1 tablespoon (15 g) minced garlic

1 tablespoon (15 ml) lemon juice

1 tablespoon (15 ml) olive oil

Salt and pepper

DIRECTIONS:

Strain the excess liquid from the yogurt by pouring the yogurt into the center of several folded layers of cheesecloth, tying it off, and suspending it over a bowl. I use the handle of a wooden spoon to tie my cheesecloth to and then rest each end of the spoon over the edge of a mixing bowl. Let sit for a few hours.

In a bowl, combine the strained yogurt, cucumber, dill, garlic, lemon juice, oil, and salt and pepper to taste.

Keep refrigerated in an airtight container until ready to use. This should keep for about 1 week.

YIELD: JUST OVER 2 CUPS (480 G)

Thai Peanut Sauce

A very simple sauce that is great for dipping, pouring, and serving over pasta, and especially good slathered all over the Thai-Inspired Black Bean Tofu and Potato Patties on page 38.

INGREDIENTS:

½ cup (128 g) peanut butter

½ cup (120 ml) peanut oil

⅓ cup (33 g) chopped scallion

2 tablespoons (30 ml) soy sauce or tamari

1 teaspoon dried red pepper flakes

DIRECTIONS:

Combine the peanut butter, oil, scallion, soy sauce, and red pepper flakes in a blender and purée until smooth.

YIELD: JUST OVER 1 CUP (240 G)

CHAPTER 12

BUNS AND BREADS

'CAUSE YOU HAVE TO EAT YOUR BURGER ON SOMETHING, RIGHT?

- Plain White Buns
- 50/50 Flatbread
- Simple Biscuits
- Rustica Buns
- Molasses Buns
- Sweet Potato Buns
- Bagel Buns
- Agave Wheat Buns

Plain White Buns

Plain. White. Buns.

INGREDIENTS:

1 cup (235 ml) plain soymilk

½ cup (120 ml) water

¼ cup (56 g) nondairy butter

4½ cups (563 g) all-purpose flour, divided

¼ ounce (7 g) quick-rise yeast

2 tablespoons (25 g) sugar

1½ teaspoons salt

Equivalent of 2 eggs*

I have made this with flax eggs, tofu eggs, and Ener-G. The best buns were with the Ener-G. The others tasted fine, but didn't puff up as much.

SERVING SUGGESTION

You honestly can't go wrong serving any of the burgers in this book on these buns. My favorites include the All-American Burger (page 82) and the Sunday Afternoon Grillers (page 98).

DIRECTIONS:

Line 2 baking sheets with parchment or a silicone baking mat.

In a saucepan or a microwave-safe bowl, combine the soymilk, water, and butter, and heat just until the butter is melted. In the microwave, I do this in about 1 minute. Set aside.

In a large bowl, combine half of the flour and the yeast, sugar, and salt.

Add the soymilk mixture to the flour and mix well, then add the egg replacer.

After well incorporated, mix in the remaining flour ½ cup (62 g) at a time.

Once all of the flour has been added, and the dough begins to form into a large mass, turn it out onto a floured surface and knead for 5 to 8 minutes, until smooth and elastic.

Divide into 8 equal pieces. Roll each piece into a smooth ball. Place on the baking sheets, 4 per sheet, and press down to flatten a little (like a disc, instead of a ball). Cover loosely and let rise for 1 hour.

Preheat the oven to 400°F (200°C, or gas mark 6).

Bake for 12 to 14 minutes, or until golden on top.

Let cool for 5 minutes on the pans before transferring to racks to cool completely.

YIELD: 8 BUNS

50/50 Flatbread

SOY
FREE

These easy flatbreads make a great stand-in for pitas, and work well as a transportation device to get some of those yummy Middle Eastern–influenced burgers directly into your mouth!

INGREDIENTS:

1½ cups (180 g) whole wheat flour

1½ cups (188 g) all-purpose flour

1 tablespoon (18 g) sea salt

1 ¼ cups (295 ml) water

DIRECTIONS:

Combine the flours and salt in a large bowl. Slowly add the water.

Mix with your hands until you get a nice big dough ball. Knead for a few minutes.

Divide into 16 equal pieces. Press each piece flat (about the size of a small pancake).

Using a dry, nonstick pan, cook each piece, one at a time, over high heat for 1½ to 2 minutes on each side.

If you have a gas stove, turn on an extra burner. After cooking in the pan, using tongs, place the flatbread on the open flame for a few seconds. It will puff up and deflate quickly. Repeat on the other side.

Stack on a plate, under a dish towel to keep warm, until all the breads are done.

YIELD: 16 FLATBREADS

SERVING SUGGESTION

These flatbreads are a great carrier for your Pizza Burgers (page 72) or any of the Middle Eastern burgers from chapter 4.

RECIPE NOTE

For another variation, add garlic and different herbs to dress up these little flatbreads.

Simple Biscuits

These are not Grandma's fluffy buttermilk biscuits. They are much more dense. But they hold a Green Castle Slider (page 87) nicely, and if you have them with breakfast, they won't get too soggy when soaked in gravy.

INGREDIENTS:

2 cups (240 g) whole wheat pastry flour

2 cups (250 g) all-purpose flour

2½ cups (590 ml) water

1 tablespoon (15 g) baking powder

1 tablespoon (15 ml) vegetable oil

½ teaspoon sea salt

3 tablespoons (63 g) agave nectar

½ cup (112 g) nondairy butter, melted

DIRECTIONS:

Preheat the oven to 450°F (230°C, or gas mark 8). Coat 2 baking sheets with butter-flavored cooking spray.

In a large bowl, combine the flours, water, baking powder, oil, salt, and agave and mix well.

Drop ice cream scoop–size mounds of dough onto the prepared baking sheets.

Bake for 10 minutes, remove from the oven, and brush on the melted butter.

Return to the oven and bake for 5 minutes longer.

YIELD: 16 BISCUITS

SERVING SUGGESTION

Serve these up with any breakfast burger from Chapter 2, especially the Chicken Fried Steak Burger on page 25.

Rustica Buns

SOY FREE

Okay, so the name is a little goofy. But these buns are really rustic looking . . . and tasting. They are hard and dry on the outside, with nooks and crannies revealing the soft orange inside. Yummy!

INGREDIENTS:

½ cup (60 g) chickpea flour

1½ cups (188 g) all-purpose flour, plus more for coating

¼ ounce (7 g) quick-rise yeast

½ teaspoon baking powder

½ teaspoon baking soda

¼ teaspoon salt

¼ cup (28 g) finely chopped sun-dried tomato pieces

2 cloves garlic, minced

2 tablespoons (30 ml) extra-virgin olive oil

½ cup (120 ml) water, plus more if needed

SERVING SUGGESTION

I enjoy these buns with all sorts of burgers, even on their own with melted, non-dairy butter, but my favorite way is with the Couscous Pantry Burgers on page 71.

DIRECTIONS:

In a mixing bowl, combine the chickpea flour, 1½ cups (188 g) all-purpose flour, yeast, baking powder, baking soda, and salt.

Add the tomatoes, garlic, and olive oil, and stir to combine.

Add the ½ cup (120 ml) water and knead well. Add more water, if needed, 1 tablespoon (15 ml) at a time, until a smooth, firm dough ball is formed. Knead for a few minutes, until uniform.

Divide into 4 equal pieces. Form each piece into a ball and then flatten slightly.

Pat a bit of all-purpose flour onto each bun to coat. Place on an oiled baking sheet. Cover loosely and let rise for 1 hour.

Preheat the oven to 350°F (180°C or gas mark 4).

Bake for 10 to 12 minutes, or until you see cracks forming on the tops.

YIELD: 4 BUNS

Molasses Buns

Sweet and soft, these buns work nicely with almost all of the burgers in the book, especially the breakfast burgers and the Seitanic Stuffer on page 100.

INGREDIENTS:

¼ ounce (7 g) active dry yeast

1 tablespoon (12 g) sugar

¼ cup (60 ml) warm water, plus more if needed

4 cups (500 g) all-purpose flour

2 teaspoons baking soda

2 teaspoons baking powder

1 teaspoon salt

1 cup (235 ml) soymilk

½ cup (112 g) nondairy butter, melted

¼ cup (88 g) molasses

1 teaspoon oil

DIRECTIONS:

In a small bowl, stir the yeast and sugar into the ¼ cup (60 ml) warm water. Let sit for 10 minutes, until foamy.

In a large mixing bowl, combine the flour, baking soda, baking powder, and salt.

In a separate bowl, combine the yeast mixture, soymilk, butter, and molasses.

Add the wet ingredients to the dry and knead until a soft, elastic dough is formed, adding more water, 1 tablespoon (15 ml) at a time, if needed.

Knead for about 10 minutes. Form into a ball.

Coat very lightly with the oil and cover with plastic wrap. Let rise for 45 minutes to 1 hour.

Preheat the oven to 425°F (220°C, or gas mark 7). Line a baking sheet with parchment or a silicone baking mat.

Punch down the dough and divide into 8 pieces, roll into balls, and flatten into a bun shape. Place on the prepared baking sheet and let sit for about 10 minutes.

Bake for 12 to 14 minutes, or until just beginning to brown.

YIELD: 8 BUNS

Sweet Potato Buns

These soft and slightly sweet buns take potato rolls to a whole new level and remind us of why we make our own bread.

INGREDIENTS:

1 large sweet potato or yam

½ ounce (14 g) active dry yeast

2 teaspoons sugar

½ cup (120 ml) warm water

¼ cup (56 g) nondairy butter, melted, plus more for brushing

1 cup (235 ml) soymilk

2 tablespoons (42 g) agave nectar

4 cups (500 g) all-purpose flour, plus more if needed

1 teaspoon salt

SERVING SUGGESTION

These soft rolls work well on almost any burger, especially the Masa Masala Burger (page 59).

DIRECTIONS:

Bring a pot of lightly salted water to a boil.

Peel and cut the sweet potato into chunks and boil until mushy.

Meanwhile, stir the yeast and sugar into the warm water. Let sit for 10 minutes, or until doubled in size.

Drain the potatoes. Return to the pot, and mash.

Add the ¼ cup (56 g) butter, soymilk, and agave nectar. Mash until very, very smooth, with as few lumps as possible.

In a separate, large mixing bowl, combine the 4 cups (500 g) flour and salt.

Add the yeast mixture to the flour and salt and stir to combine.

Add the potato mixture and knead for 8 to 10 minutes, adding more flour if the dough is too sticky.

Knead until a soft, elastic dough ball forms. (I knead it right in the bowl.)

Cover loosely with a dish towel, and let rise for 1 hour.

Preheat the oven to 350°F (180°C, or gas mark 4). Line 2 baking sheets with parchment or a silicone baking mat.

Punch down the dough and knead for about 2 minutes. Add a little more flour if the dough is too sticky.

Divide into 12 equal pieces, roll into balls, and flatten slightly. Place 6 on each baking sheet.

Bake for 12 to 15 minutes.

Remove from the oven, brush with extra melted butter, and bake for 5 minutes longer, or until golden brown on top.

YiELD: 12 BUNS

Bagel Buns SOY FREE

Shiny bagel buns are a great way to serve up your breakfast burgers!

INGREDIENTS:

¼ ounce (7 g) active dry yeast

1 tablespoon (12 g) sugar

1 cup (235 ml) plus ¼ to ½ cup (60 to 120 ml) warm water, divided

4 cups (500 g) all-purpose flour

1½ teaspoons salt

1 tablespoon (15 ml) vegetable oil

RECIPE NOTE

If you'd like, add poppy seeds, sesame seeds, or—my favorite—everything (garlic, poppy seeds, and coarse sea salt) to your bagels after you boil them but before you bake them by placing them face down in a shallow dish of seeds and then baking face up, and then flipping as directed above.

DIRECTIONS:

Stir the yeast and sugar into 1 cup (235 ml) warm water and let sit for 10 minutes.

In a mixing bowl, combine the flour and salt.

Add the yeast mixture and oil. Knead for about 10 minutes, adding more of the remaining water, 2 tablespoons (30 ml) at a time, until you get a smooth, elastic dough ball.

Lightly coat with the vegetable oil, cover with plastic wrap, and let rise for 1 hour.

Punch down the dough. Knead for 2 to 3 minutes.

Divide the dough into 8 equal pieces. Roll into a ball and flatten each ball into a bun shape.

Once again, lightly coat with oil, cover, and let rest for 20 minutes.

Meanwhile, bring a large pot of water to a boil and preheat the oven to 425°F (220°C, or gas mark 7). Line a baking sheet with parchment or a silicone baking mat.

Add 2 or 3 bagel buns to the boiling water and boil for 1 minute, flip over, and boil for 1 minute longer.

Remove from the water with a slotted spoon, let dry for about 1 minute, and place on the prepared baking sheet. Repeat until all 8 bagels have been boiled.

Bake the bagels for 10 minutes, remove from the oven, flip, and bake 10 minutes longer.

YIELD: 8 BAGELS

Agave Wheat Buns

Sweet and soft wheat buns for all of your burger needs.

INGREDIENTS:

½ ounce (14 g) quick-rise yeast

1½ cups (188 g) all-purpose flour, plus more as needed

1½ cups (180 g) whole wheat flour

1 teaspoon salt

½ cup (120 ml) nondairy milk

¼ cup (84 g) agave nectar

¼ cup (56 g) nondairy butter, melted

½ cup (120 ml) water

SERVING SUGGESTION

They go especially great with the Scarborough Fair Tofu Burger (page 84) and the Earth Burger (page 157).

DIRECTIONS:

In a large mixing bowl, combine the yeast, 1½ cups (188 g) all-purpose flour, the whole wheat flour, and the salt.

In a microwave-safe bowl, combine the milk, agave, butter, and water. Warm in the microwave to 110° to 120°F (43° to 48°C), about 1 minute. This step is necessary to activate the yeast.

Slowly add the wet ingredients to the dry and knead into a soft, elastic dough. If your dough is too sticky, add more flour, 1 tablespoon (8 g) at a time. Cover the dough with a dish towel and let sit for 10 minutes. You probably won't see a noticeable rise here, but that's okay.

Line a baking sheet with parchment or a silicone mat.

Punch down the dough, and break into 8 equal pieces. Form into bun shapes, place on the prepared baking sheet, cover with a dish towel, and let rise for about 45 minutes, pr until doubled in size.

Preheat the oven to 350°F (180°C, or gas mark 4).

Bake for about 25 minutes, or until golden brown.

YIELD: 8 BUNS

CHAPTER 13

SiDES AND SALADS

TASTY TiDBiTS TO COMPLETE YOUR MEAL

- Sweet Potato Fries
- Fried Zucchini
- Basic Mac Salad
- Fiesta Mac Salad
- Papa's Spicy Mac Salad
- Cedar-Smoked Tofu and Pasta Salad with Chipotle Roasted Red Pepper Dressing

- Mediterranean Orzo Salad
- Smoky Potato Salad
- Creamy BBQ Coleslaw
- Cilantro Lime Rice
- Traditional Boiled Seitan

Sweet Potato Fries

WHEAT FREE **SOY FREE**

These fries would pretty much go fantastically with any recipe in this book, though one of my favorite pairings is the Edamame Burger on page 46, where these fries happen to be pictured.

INGREDIENTS:

1 large or 2 small yams or sweet potatoes

Salt and pepper

Olive oil, for drizzling

DIRECTIONS:

Preheat the oven to 350°F (180°C, or gas mark 4). Line a baking sheet with foil. Line a plate with paper towels.

Wash and pat dry the potatoes. I leave the skin on, but if you prefer, peel them.

Cut the potatoes into "fry" shapes: wedges, steak fries, skinny fries . . . it's totally a personal preference. Arrange the fries on the prepared baking sheet. Sprinkle desired amount of seasoning onto the fries, and liberally drizzle olive oil all over them.

Bake for 20 minutes, then rotate them on the baking sheet and bake for 20 minutes longer.

Transfer to the plate to absorb excess oil.

YIELD: 2 TO 4 SERVINGS

Fried Zucchini SOY FREE

I find it absolutely meditative and sexy to stand in the kitchen and hand chop vegetables. There is a sensuality to it that is simply unexplainable. First the washing and the drying of freshly bought produce, and then the power of the sharp blade slicing and dicing it into little pieces of goodness that will make the meal.

One evening I was very ready to hand slice some zucchini and even got out a hand grater to shred some for burgers, but for some reason, I wanted to try out the slicing attachment on my food processor. I had had the thing for more than two years and had never used that attachment. So I used it. Dang if it didn't slice that zucchini into a bajillion little discs in a matter of 3 seconds! Whoa.

I might just have to use it a little more often . . . seriously, what could be sexier than power tools?

INGREDIENTS:

2 or 3 zucchini, sliced into rounds

1 cup (125 g) all-purpose flour

½ teaspoon paprika

½ teaspoon cayenne pepper

½ teaspoon dried parsley

Salt and pepper

Oil, for frying

SERVING SUGGESTION

Serve as an alternative to French fries with your next Sunday Afternoon Griller (page 98).

DIRECTIONS:

Place the zukes, flour, paprika, cayenne, parsley, and salt and pepper to taste in a large zipper-seal bag and shake until you get a nice coating on each piece. Line a plate with paper towels.

Preheat ¼ inch (6 mm) oil in a cast-iron skillet over high heat. The oil is ready when a piece of dough dropped into it sizzles immediately. Fry these puppies until golden, 1 to 2 minutes per side. Make sure you don't overcrowd the pan.

Remove from the oil with a slotted spoon and transfer to the plate to absorb excess oil.

Pop 'em back into the bag for a fresh coating of the flour mixture.

Meanwhile, add a little bit more oil to the pan and let it heat back up.

Then, for the second fry. This time, cook a little longer on each side, to get that yummy golden brown color. After the second fry, it's back to the draining plate.

Serve with Chunky Marinara (page 188) for dipping.

YIELD: 4 SERVINGS

Basic Mac Salad

Plain and simple and perfect for pot lucks and get-togethers.

INGREDIENTS:

1 pound (454 g) pasta of your choice

1 cup (225 g) vegan mayonnaise, store-bought or homemade (page 191)

1 cup (160 g) diced onion

¼ cup (25 g) imitation bacon bits, store-bought or homemade (page 185)

¼ cup (28 g) diced scallion

2 tablespoons (30 g) Dijon mustard

1 teaspoon garlic powder

1 teaspoon onion powder

Salt and pepper

DIRECTIONS:

Cook the pasta in lightly salted water according to package directions.

Drain and let cool. Or cool off the pasta quickly by running under cold water.

Mix in the mayonnaise, onion, bacon bits, scallion, mustard, garlic powder, onion powder, and salt and pepper to taste and refrigerate until ready to serve.

YIELD: 8 SERVINGS

RECIPE NOTE

Chopped celery, shredded carrots, cashews, chopped red bell peppers, and pickle relish are all wonderful add-ins.

Fiesta Mac Salad

Yes, another mac salad. Can you tell that I am addicted to mac salad? It's just that mac salad and burgers go together almost as well as peanut butter and jelly do.

INGREDIENTS:

1 pound (454 g) elbow macaroni, cooked in salted water according to package instructions

1 cup (16 g) chopped fresh cilantro

1 red onion, diced

12 ounces (340 g) fire-roasted red peppers (I use jarred, packed in water)

½ cup (112 g) vegan mayonnaise, store-bought or homemade (page 191)

¾ cup (180 g) nondairy sour cream, store-bought or homemade (page 191)

1 packet (2 tablespoons, or 16 g) taco seasoning, store-bought or homemade (page 184)

1 teaspoon cayenne pepper

1 teaspoon ground cumin

Salt and pepper

DIRECTIONS:

Drain and cool the prepared pasta. Transfer to a large bowl.

In a separate bowl, combine the cilantro, onion, peppers, mayonnaise, sour cream, taco seasoning, cayenne pepper, cumin, and salt and pepper to taste. Add to the pasta and toss to combine.

Refrigerate until ready to serve.

YIELD: 8 SERVINGS

SERVING SUGGESTION

This one pairs particularly well with the Mexican-style burgers in Chapter 7.

Papa's Spicy Mac Salad

My papa likes things really spicy—that's where I get it from! I made this mac salad for him.

FOR DRESSING:

1 cup (224 g) vegan mayonnaise, store-bought or homemade (page 191)

⅓ cup (80 ml) olive oil

1 tablespoon (15 ml) apple cider vinegar

2 teaspoons cayenne pepper

2 tablespoons (16 g) garlic powder

2 tablespoons (16 g) onion powder

2 tablespoons (30 g) brown mustard

2 tablespoons (42 g) agave nectar

1 tablespoon (7 g) paprika

Salt and pepper

FOR SALAD:

1 pound (454 g) elbow macaroni, cooked in salted water according to package directions

1 recipe Dressing (above)

12 ounces (340 g) roasted red peppers, cut into thin strips

14 ounces (392 g) artichoke hearts, roughly chopped

2 cups (60 g) fresh spinach, cut into chiffonade

10 large fresh basil leaves, cut into chiffonade

DIRECTIONS:

To make the dressing: Whisk all the ingredients together. Refrigerate until ready to use.

To make the salad: In a large bowl, toss the pasta with the dressing.

Add the red peppers, artichoke hearts, spinach, and basil. Toss until well combined.

Cover and refrigerate for several hours before serving.

YIELD: 8 SERVINGS

Cedar-Smoked Tofu and Pasta Salad with Chipotle Roasted Red Pepper Dressing

This salad not only goes great with burgers, but it also goes fabulously with just about anything!

INGREDIENTS:

1 pound (454 g) pasta of your choice

1 pound (454 g) extra-firm smoked tofu (you can buy it already smoked or make your own, see note), cut into bite-size chunks

1 cup (224 g) vegan mayonnaise, store-bought or homemade (page 191)

1 teaspoon garlic powder

1 teaspoon onion powder

1 teaspoon chipotle powder

1 teaspoon chili powder

12 ounces (340 g) roasted red peppers, thinly sliced

14 ounces (392 g) spinach, drained if using canned or cut into chiffonade if fresh

Salt and pepper

DIRECTIONS:

Cook the pasta in lightly salted water according to package directions.

Drain and let cool. Or cool off the pasta quickly by running under cold water.

In a large bowl, combine the tofu, mayonnaise, garlic powder, onion powder, chipotle powder, chili powder, red peppers, spinach, and salt and pepper to taste.

Add the pasta and toss to combine.

Refrigerate until ready to eat.

YIELD: 8 SERVINGS

RECIPE NOTE

To make your own smoked tofu, try this very simple technique. First, buy a food-safe cedar plank. Soak it in water for at least 1 hour, more if you have time. Preheat the oven to 200°F (100°C, or gas mark ¼). Slice a block of extra-firm tofu and arrange on the plank. Place the plank in the oven and bake for 90 minutes to 3 hours. The outside of the tofu will turn brown and become firm. The inside will stay moist and chewy. Use the tofu in any recipe.

Mediterranean Orzo Salad

This pasta salad is light and tasty without being weighed down in a heavy mayo-based dressing. If you don't have any spinach on hand, any sort of leaf lettuce will work fine.

INGREDIENTS:

1 pound (454 g) orzo, cooked in salted water according to package directions

14 ounces (392 g) extra-firm tofu, drained, pressed, and cubed*

¼ cup (60 ml) olive oil

12 sun-dried tomatoes, chopped

2 cups (60 g) fresh spinach, cut into chiffonade

2 cloves garlic, finely diced

1 tablespoon (8 g) onion powder

12 large leaves fresh basil, cut into chiffonade

12 kalamata olives, pitted and chopped

Salt and pepper

If you have a favorite tofu feta recipe, use that.

DIRECTIONS:

Combine all the ingredients and mix well.

Serve hot or cold.

YIELD: 4 TO 6 SERVINGS

SERVING SUGGESTION

Serve up warm or cold alongside some of the "Burgers from the Boot" in Chapter 5.

Smoky Potato Salad

What would a burger book be if there weren't a recipe for potato salad in it?

INGREDIENTS:

1 ¼ pounds (568 g) red potatoes

1 small yellow or red onion, diced

2 stalks celery, chopped (optional)

2 tablespoons (4 g) chopped fresh parsley

¼ teaspoon liquid smoke

1 cup (224 g) vegan mayonnaise, store-bought or homemade (page 191)

1 tablespoon (15 ml) lemon juice

2 tablespoons (30 g) nondairy sour cream, store-bought or homemade (page 191)

2 tablespoons (13 g) imitation bacon bits, store-bought or homemade (page 185, optional)

Salt and pepper

DIRECTIONS:

Wash the potatoes and cut into bite-size chunks. I like to leave the skin on, but peel them if that's how you roll.

Bring a pot of salted water to a boil. Add the potatoes and cook for 7 to 10 minutes, or until fork-tender. Drain and let cool completely.

In a large bowl, combine the onion, celery, parsley, liquid smoke, mayonnaise, lemon juice, sour cream, and bacon bits. Fold into the potatoes after they have completely cooled, taking care not to break the potato pieces. Season with salt and pepper to taste.

Refrigerate until ready to serve.

YiELD: 8 SERViNGS

SERViNG SUGGESTiON

This side is a fabulous accompaniment to the Basic Black Bean BBQ Burger (page 90), the Oktoberfest Kraut Burger (page 165), and basically any other burger you've got on board.

Creamy BBQ Coleslaw

WHEAT FREE

This coleslaw adds a tangy, sassy twist to the classic coleslaw.

INGREDIENTS:

1 cup (224 g) vegan mayonnaise, store-bought or homemade (page 191)

⅓ cup (80 ml) barbecue sauce, store-bought or homemade (page 183)

⅓ cup (116 g) agave nectar

2 tablespoons (30 ml) apple cider vinegar

Salt and pepper

1 head cabbage, cored and shredded

DIRECTIONS:

In a large bowl, combine the mayonnaise, barbecue sauce, agave, vinegar, and salt and pepper to taste.

Add the cabbage and toss to coat.

Refrigerate until ready to serve.

YIELD: 12 SERVINGS

SERVING SUGGESTION

This tastes great piled onto the Pulled Pork Sammy (page 178) or on its own as a side dish.

Cilantro Lime Rice

I wanted to recreate a rice that tasted as much like the rice they make at Chipotle Mexican Grill. This is what I came up with.

INGREDIENTS:

2 tablespoons (28 g) nondairy butter

1 ⅓ cups (253 g) uncooked basmati rice

2 cups (470 ml) water

1 teaspoon salt

Juice of 2 limes

¼ cup (4 g) finely chopped fresh cilantro

SERVING SUGGESTION

This is another great side dish to serve up alongside the Mexican-inspired burgers, like Sarah's Southwest Burger on page 129.

DIRECTIONS:

In a pot with a tight-fitting lid, melt the butter over low heat.

Add the rice, and stir to coat. Cook for about 1 minute to lightly toast the rice.

Add the water, salt, and lime juice. Bring to a boil. Reduce to a simmer and cover.

Simmer, covered, for 20 to 25 minutes, or until the rice is tender and the liquid is absorbed. Stir occasionally to prevent the rice from sticking or scorching on the bottom of the pan.

Fluff with a fork and fold in the chopped cilantro.

YIELD: ABOUT 3 CUPS (495 G)

Traditional Boiled Seitan

This plain and simple seitan has a neutral beefy flavor and works well in recipes calling for prepared seitan.

FOR BOILING BROTH:

10 cups (2.35 L) water

2 cups (470 ml) soy sauce

10 cloves garlic, chopped in half

5 whole bay leaves

3 (2-inch, or 5-cm) slices fresh ginger or 1 hand, chopped into chunks

FOR SEITAN DOUGH:

1 cup (144 g) vital wheat gluten flour

5 cups (600 g) whole wheat flour

2½ cups (588 ml) water

½ cup (32 g) chopped fresh parsley

3 scallions, whites only, finely chopped

1 teaspoon garlic powder

1 teaspoon onion powder

1 to 3 teaspoons freshly cracked pepper, to taste

DIRECTIONS:

To make the broth: Combine all the broth ingredients in a large stockpot and bring to a simmer.

To make the seitan dough: In a large mixing bowl, combine the flours, then slowly add the water and form into a stiff dough. Knead the dough about 70 times. You can do it right in the bowl. Let rest for 20 minutes.

After resting, take the dough, in the bowl, to the sink and cover with water. Knead the dough until the water becomes milky, then drain off the water and repeat. Do this 10 to 12 times. By the tenth or twelfth time, the dough will feel and look like the consistency of brains, but the water will still be a little milky.

After the last rinse, add the parsley, scallions, garlic powder, onion powder, and pepper. Mix thoroughly by hand.

Divide the dough in half. Place 1 piece of dough in the center of a large piece of cheesecloth and roll tightly into a log shape. Tie the ends to secure. Repeat with the other piece.

Place both logs in the broth and simmer for 90 minutes.

Remove from the broth and set on a plate to cool. Unwrap. If the cheesecloth is sticking, run under some water, and it should come off easily.

You can store the seitan in the refrigerator wrapped in foil or in a plastic container. To keep it really moist, place some of the broth in the container. Will keep in the fridge for about 2 weeks, or indefinitely in the freezer.

YIELD: ABOUT 4 POUNDS (1816 G)

CHAPTER 14

A FEW DESSERTS

A FEW SWEET TREATS
TO FINISH OFF YOUR MEAL

- Lemon Poppy Seed Cake
- Cherry Oatmeal Chocolate Chip Cookies
- Blueberry Mango Upside-Down Shortcake
- Espresso Chocolate Chip Cake

Lemon Poppy Seed Cake

This is my go-to bake sale recipe! The recipe makes a lot, because I always make these in bulk. Think about hosting your own bake sale to raise money for local animal rescues. Visit www.veganbakesale.org for more information.

INGREDIENTS:

nonstick spray

2 containers (12 ounces, or 340 g) lemon soy yogurt (plain or vanilla will work, too)

1 cup (235 ml) plain or vanilla soymilk

1 cup (235 ml) canola oil

1 tablespoon (15 ml) vanilla extract

1 teaspoon lemon extract

Zest and juice of 1 lemon

½ cup (115 g) nondairy sour cream, store-bought or homemade (page 191)

2 tablespoons (16 g) poppy seeds

5 cups (600 g) all-purpose flour

2 cups (400 g) sugar

3 tablespoons (24 g) cornstarch

1 tablespoon (15 g) baking powder

1 tablespoon (15 g) baking soda

1 teaspoon salt

DIRECTIONS:

Preheat the oven to 350°F (180°C, or gas mark 4). Coat 6 mini loaf pans with nonstick spray.

In a large mixing bowl, combine the yogurt, soymilk, oil, vanilla, lemon extract, lemon zest and juice, and sour cream.

In a separate bowl, mix together the poppy seeds, flour, sugar, cornstarch, baking powder, baking soda, and salt. Add the dry ingredients to the wet and stir to combine. The mixture will be thick, not runny.

Fill the loaf pans about two-thirds full.

Bake for about 45 minutes, or until a toothpick inserted into the center comes out clean. Let cool, then turn out onto cooling racks.

YIELD: 6 MINI LOAVES

Cherry Oatmeal Chocolate Chip Cookies

I liken these to a cross between a macaroon and a chocolate chip cookie, with bits of tart cherries thrown in for good measure!

INGREDIENTS:

1 cup (224 g) nondairy butter, softened

¾ cup (150 g) sugar

¾ cup (165 g) packed brown sugar

¼ cup (84 g) agave nectar

1 container (6 ounces, or 170 g) vanilla soy yogurt

1 teaspoon vanilla extract

1 cup (125 g) all-purpose flour

1 cup (112 g) coconut flour

1 cup (80 g) quick-cooking oats

1 teaspoon baking soda

1 teaspoon baking powder

½ teaspoon salt

1 cup (120 g) dried cherries or any dried fruit

1 cup (176 g) nondairy chocolate chips

½ cup (60 g) shredded coconut

DIRECTIONS:

Preheat the oven to 350°F (180°C, or gas mark 4). Line 2 baking sheets with parchment or silicone baking mats.

In a large mixing bowl, beat together the butter, sugars, agave, yogurt, and vanilla.

In a separate bowl, mix together the flours, oats, baking soda, baking powder, and salt.

Add the dry ingredients to the wet and stir to combine. Fold in the cherries, chocolate chips, and coconut.

Form into balls using about ⅓ cup (65 g) of dough per ball, slightly flatten, and place on the prepared baking sheet about 2 inches (5 cm) apart.

Bake for 12 to 15 minutes, or until lightly browned.

Allow to cool completely before transferring to cooling racks.

YIELD: 24 COOKIES

Blueberry Mango Upside-Down Shortcake

I think the name says it all.

INGREDIENTS:

1 mango, peeled, seeded, and cubed

1 cup (145 g) fresh blueberries

2 cups (400 g) sugar, divided

2 cups (250 g) all-purpose flour

1 teaspoon arrowroot powder

½ teaspoon baking powder

½ teaspoon baking soda

¼ teaspoon salt

1 container (6 ounces, or 170 g) plain or vanilla soy yogurt

4 ounces (112 g) applesauce

¼ cup (60 ml) nondairy milk

¼ cup (60 ml) canola or other mild-flavored vegetable oil

2 teaspoons vanilla extract

FOR ICING (OPTIONAL):

1 cup (120 g) powdered sugar

3 tablespoons (45 ml) soy or other nondairy milk

DIRECTIONS:

Preheat the oven to 350°F (180°C, or gas mark 4). If you have a really good nonstick muffin pan, use it. I don't like to use paper cups for these, but you can if you want to.

In a bowl, combine the mango, blueberries, and ½ cup (100 g) of the sugar. Set aside.

In a separate bowl, sift together the remaining 1½ cups (300 g) sugar, flour, arrowroot powder, baking powder, baking soda, and salt.

In another bowl, combine the yogurt, applesauce, milk, oil, and vanilla. Add the wet ingredients to the dry and stir to combine.

Divide the fruit evenly among the 12 muffin cups. Spoon the batter evenly on top of the fruit.

Bake for about 20 minutes, or until golden brown.

Remove from the oven and let cool for a few minutes.

Invert onto a baking sheet, and allow the shortcakes to naturally fall out of the pan.

To make the icing: Combine the confectioners' sugar and soymilk in a bowl and whisk until smooth. Drizzle over the shortcakes.

YIELD: 12 SHORTCAKES

Espresso Chocolate Chip Cake

This cake is perfect for gift giving, bake sales, or simply to eat all yourself!

INGREDIENTS:

1 container (6 ounces, or 170 g) vanilla or plain soy yogurt

1 cup (235 ml) canola oil

1 tablespoon (15 ml) vanilla extract

1 tablespoon (15 ml) chocolate extract (or more vanilla)

2 cups (400 g) sugar

2 tablespoons (40 g) molasses

½ cup (120 ml) coffee-flavored liqueur

1 cup (235 ml) vanilla or plain soymilk

½ cup (115 g) instant coffee crystals

3½ cups (438 g) all-purpose flour

1 cup (120 g) whole wheat pastry flour

½ cup (40 g) cocoa powder

2 teaspoons baking powder

2 teaspoons baking soda

2 tablespoons (16 g) cornstarch

1 teaspoon salt

1½ cups (263 g) nondairy chocolate chips

DIRECTIONS:

Preheat the oven to 350°F (180°C, or gas mark 4). Coat 6 mini loaf pans with nonstick spray.

In a large bowl, combine the yogurt, oil, vanilla, chocolate extract, sugar, molasses, liqueur, and soymilk.

In a separate bowl, sift together the coffee crystals, flours, cocoa powder, baking powder, baking soda, cornstarch, and salt.

Add the dry ingredients to the wet, and stir to combine. Fold in the chocolate chips.

Fill the loaf pans about two-thirds full.

Bake for 30 to 45 minutes, or until a toothpick inserted into the center comes out clean.

YIELD: 6 MINI LOAVES

SERVING SUGGESTION

If you're feeling naughty, this cake makes a great breakfast treat! It also makes a nice after dinner treat with a double shot of espresso or a tall glass of vanilla rice milk.

SOURCES

I try my best to source local, organic produce. I tremendously enjoy strolling through a farmers' market, talking with the vendors, and finding the best produce from local farmers that I know need the support. It's just a bonus that these open-air markets usually have much lower prices than supermarkets do.

When it comes to markets, however, I am a lucky gal. I live within an hour's drive of two Whole Foods, two Henry's, two Mother's, four Trader Joe's, Sprouts, and Fresh and Easy, not to mention the other international, specialty, and traditional markets in the area. If you live near these types of stores, most ingredients can be found there.

I realize, however, that not everyone is so fortunate . . . thank goodness for the Internet! Almost any hard-to-find ingredient can be found there.

Here are a few of my favorite sites:

bobsredmill.com for flours and grains. I almost exclusively use Bob's vital wheat gluten flour, coconut flour, gluten-free biscuit and baking mix, and TVP.

thespicehouse.com for herbs and spices that are hand ground in small batches.

foodfightgrocery.com for hanything your heart desires! From cheese to candy, this 100 percent vegan store in the famous Portland vegan mini mall will knock your socks off!

And, of course, you can simply enter what you're looking for into Google and you are sure to find hundreds of sources.

TESTER RECOGNITION

I couldn't have done it without you.

There is no way I could have created this book without the help of all of the testers. Their hard work, tips and tricks, and helpful feedback made all of this possible. Thanks, ladies! You are VERY appreciated!

Extra special thanks to Liz Wyman, who tested more than forty burgers! What a gal!

LIZ WYMAN ● Stoke-on-Trent, England ● veganefcliz.wordpress.com

Favorite Burgers: "I think I might have to say the *Sunday Afternoon Grillers* because even out of the freezer, they stayed so moist, but for a real comfort food burger, I'd have to say the *Savory Noodle Kugel Burger*."

TAMARA HARDEN ● Puyallup, Washington ● photoblog.com/veganess

Favorite Burger-Making Tip: "Make them small, and not too thin, or they will fall apart, even when making the bean burgers. And fry until crisp . . . they stay together much better."

LISA COULSON ● Brooklyn, New York ● pandawithcookie.etsy.com

Favorite Burgers: "I think the *Seitanic Stuffers* and the *Earth Burgers*. There are so many that have been good, but I have made both of these more than once."

AMANDA SOMERVILLE ● Bartlett, Illinois ● theppk.com

Favorite Burger-Making Tip: "Err on the small side rather than huge burgers to help them cook all the way through." Favorite Burger: *Cinco de Mayo Burgers*

MARY WORRELL ● Norfolk, Virginia ● veganhamptonroads.com

Favorite Burger-Making Tip: "I love to put the uncooked (or cooked, in some cases) patties on squares of waxed paper and stack them in the freezer. Once they're firm I put them in plastic bags or vacuum pack them for the freezer. Then you can have homemade burgers all the time without the mess!"

JENNIFER SHRIER ● Huntington Beach, California

Favorite Burger: "*Ortega Burger*. These patties are filling, tasty, healthy, easy, and no fuss. These are perfect for a non-vegan, like me, who appreciates the occasional vegan meal. It makes it feasible to add a vegan meal to my weekly menu because I can use everyday 'normal' ingredients I am familiar with without having to go to the store to pick up some random vegan ingredient that I will only use once."

SHEREE' BRIT ● Santee, California ● boosveg-a-nut.blogspot.com

Favorite Burger: "I love *Sarah's Southwest Burger* and the *Aloha Teriyaki Burger*—my dad's family is from Hawaii, so I just can't help myself."

CYNDEE LEE RULE ● Trevose, Pennsylvania ● cyndeeleerule.com

Favorite Burger: "Loved *Lizzy's Lentil Daal Burger* especially. Love the spicier ones the best!"

AMANDA DICKIE ● Halifax, Canada ● notjustgreens.blogspot.com

Favorite Burger: "*Smoky Tempeh Seitanic Stuffers*! They are amazing. Seriously, I could live off of these suckers for weeks."

JAMIE COBLE ● Knoxville, Tennessee

Favorite Burger-Making Tip: "My method for making evenly sized burgers (it helps them cook evenly and be 'burger' shaped) is to use my expandable measuring cups to measure each burger, usually ¼ to ⅓ cup, and then squeeze it right out! They are perfectly round and require just a bit of patting to smoosh them down some."

Favorite Burger: "The *Deli-Style No-Tuna Melt*. It's quick, easy, and delicious! Plus, I can change it up easily by adding different spices, condiments, and veggies."

MICHELLE GRAVES ● Norristown, Pennsylvania

Favorite Burger-Making Tip: "If there was something you didn't like the first time around, it's not necessarily a lost cause. Don't be afraid to change up the ingredients to your liking, but do keep an eye on texture so they don't end up crumbly or dry. In the end, no one knows your tastes better than you."

Favorite Burgers: "*Baked Popeye Burgers* when I am watching what I eat and grilled *Bacon Cheeseburgers* when I am throwing caution to the wind. My husband is a really big fan of the *Bacon and Egg Breakfast Burgers*; in fact, he hardly ever stops hounding me to make them . . ."

JULIE FARSON ● Phoenix, Arizona ● kindkitchen.wordpress.com

Favorite Burger: "My favorite burger was the *Bacon Cheeseburger*!! Quick and easy to make, but filling and tasty."

KARYN CASPER ● Frederick, Maryland ● threepotato.blogspot.com

Favorite Burger-Making Tip: "If you knead something long enough, it will become a patty."

Favorite Burger: "*Green Castle Sliders* are my fave (so far). I just like sliders because they are small and cute."

MELISSER ELLIOTT ● San Francisco, California ● theurbanhousewife.com

Favorite Burger: "*Jalapeño Cornbread Burgers*! My husband and his non-veg brother devoured these so quickly, I feared I wouldn't get one myself! The *Ortega Burgers* are excellent, too!"

ABOUT THE AUTHOR

I am Joni Marie Newman, self-appointed **QUEEN OF VEGGIE BURGERS!** I am just a regular gal who loves to cook and bake, *especially* for friends and family. Self-taught, and still learning, I spend most of my spare time in the kitchen. I am also the co-author of *500 Vegan Recipes* and *The Complete Guide to Vegan Food Substitutions*, which I wrote along with my dear friend, Celine Steen.

When I am not in the kitchen, I really enjoy knitting, painting, wasting endless hours on the Internet, hiking with my husband and the girls, traveling, reading, and most of the other stuff regular gals enjoy.

I currently reside in Orange County, California, but before you go all *The Real Housewives of Orange County* on me, let me tell you that I live in a small cottage, with my three rescue mutts, my very handsome cat, and my extremely delicious husband, in one of the last rural towns in Southern California.

It is in this cottage that I create delicious and cruelty-free delicacies for the world to enjoy. Through my food, I hope to help people understand that *it is not necessary to murder or torture another living creature in order to have a tasty supper.*

SPECIAL THANKS

I cannot even put into words the amount of appreciation I have for those of my friends and family who have had to put up with my ridiculous burger antics over the past three and a half years.

My poor husband, Dan, has had to eat so many burgers, I thought he might explode! Thanks, baby. I know you think that I had given up on us, in favor of the mixing bowls and the computer, but I assure you, I am still deeply in love with you!

I also would like to give an *extra* special thanks to two very wonderful and talented ladies whom I have come to know and love via the virtues of the vegan Internet community. Celine Steen, of HaveCakeWillTravel.com, now one of my dearest friends and vegan partner in crime (coauthor of *500 Vegan Recipes, The Complete Guide to Vegan Food Substitutions*, and *Hearty Vegan*), has taken the gorgeous photos that grace the pages of this book. Isa Chandra Moskowitz, of *Vegan with a Vengeance, Vegan Cupcakes Take Over the World, Vegan Brunch, Veganomicon*, and *Vegan Cookies Invade Your Cookie Jar* fame, has both inspired and mentored me over the years. Ladies, you rock!

Speaking of the vegan Internet community, a very heartfelt thanks goes to all of you guys. I really feel as though I have friends all over the world. We speak to each other through our photos and our blogs. I feel I know you all personally and have a great affection for you. Without you guys, I would not be where I am today, and I certainly wouldn't have had the opportunity to write this book!

I would like to say thanks to Jen and Lars for always helping me stay positive and willingly coming over to give me an honest opinion of what I was stuffing into their bellies; to Tony and Lizzie for not complaining when I left tons of frozen burgers in their freezer every time I came over; to Sissy Krissy for being my muse when things got rough; to Sissy June and Kurt, for taking me on the most amazing "culinary" tours of Portland (even if it was mostly coffee and sweet treats from SweetPea!); and, of course, to my mommy for always telling me she was proud of me and for being, well, the perfect mom. I love you guys. I really do.

Finally, a sincere thanks to my editor and friend, Amanda Waddell, for convincing the powers that be to take a chance on a book full of burgers; to Will Kiester, Rosalind Wanke, Karen Levy, and Bradhamdesign.com: This book wouldn't exist without your faith, hard work, and talent!

INDEX